Faith is a living, daring confidence in God's grace.

MARTIN LUTHER
(1483–1546)

GRACE FROM HEAVEN

PRAYERS
of the
REFORMATION

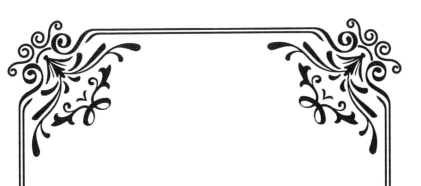

GRACE FROM HEAVEN

|

PRAYERS
of the
REFORMATION

|

Robert Elmer, Editor

LEXHAM PRESS

Grace from Heaven: Prayers of the Reformation
Prayers of the Church, edited by Robert Elmer

Copyright 2024 Robert Elmer

Lexham Press, 1313 Commercial St., Bellingham, WA 98225
LexhamPress.com

Print ISBN 9781683597407
Digital ISBN 9781683597414
Library of Congress Control Number 2023938809

Series Editor: Robert Elmer
Lexham Editorial: Elliot Ritzema
Cover Design: Jim LePage
Typesetting: Justin Marr

23 24 25 26 27 28 29 / IN / 12 11 10 9 8 7 6 5 4 3 2 1

Introduction   1

List of Authors   5

THE PRAYERS

ALIVE IN YOUR GRACE
(PRAYERS OF PRAISE)   11

*Looking to the sky, we praise your name · Jesus, your
name is sweet · Teach us in the school of praise · To
the God who is beyond comprehending · Your name is
great · Joining in the concert of praise · I pass all things
to you · No sweeter name · Let our hearts pursue you,
Lord Christ · Light up my life, Lord · No other name
comes close!*

WE SEE YOUR GOODNESS
(PRAYERS OF RECOGNITION AND THANKS)   23

*Holy Spirit, come! · May we not misuse your gifts ·
Thank you for the blessings of relationships · You only
give us what we need · May your Spirit be present as
we meet · Thank you for your gifts of grace · Help me
pray with my whole heart · Thanksgiving in a time of
persecution · I thank you, more than I can say · You
crown the year with your goodness · Thanks for the
gift of baptism*

WE PROCLAIM YOUR TRUTH
(PRAYERS OF AFFIRMATION)   35

*I believe! · I believe in repentance · I lift up my soul ·
Keep me in faith until my end · I believe the Holy Spirit
is in me · I believe all is not lost · I believe in Jesus
Christ · I would rather be in trouble than without you ·
I believe you ransomed me by your cross · I believe
in eternal life · I am in trouble—and I trust in you ·*

I believe you hear from heaven · Plant the seed that brings lifetime fruit · I believe you are coming again · I believe in the resurrection · I believe in the Holy Spirit · I believe you conquered death

We Bow before You
(Prayers of Dedication)

49

We are loaded with failings, but you invite us to yourself · Keep us working for your glory until the end · The world's disapproval does not matter · We want less of us, more of you · Give us a spirit to wear your yoke · Help us stay pure as husband and wife · Transform my tongue into something new · For your sake, Lord, transform me · May we eat for your glory · Fill this empty vessel · Rip out the worst · replace it with the best · Let your Spirit possess my heart · You have chosen us as priests · Keep us hurrying down the path · Lord, we want to serve you · Draw me close in your love · Let us belong to you completely · May we finish the race strong · I commit to you my life and future · Grant me a place under your feet · Help me to get my priorities straight · I want no other God than you · How can we find our way home? · A soldier's prayer of dedication · I embrace only you, sweet Jesus · I wholly commit myself to you · Just passing through? · Grant me a mind to know you · Keep us on the right path

No Matter the Challenge
(Prayers in Adversity)

79

Help in this trouble · You sent not a Jonah, but Jesus · As illness descends · Be glorified in my life or death · Raise us up like a grapevine · A dying prayer · Help me to do as you command · Your will is mine · We will one day sing with Simeon · On earth as it is in heaven · So great a kindness · Even when we are almost buried · Help us to continue in obedience · A prayer for patience · Lead us to your kingdom, Lord · All the help we can get · Let adversities energize my faith · Keep me on your path · You turn adversity for my good · We wait for you, Redeemer · An appeal for healing · We deserve the worst, but thank you for the best · Save us from anger and revenge

We Need Your Forgiveness (Prayers of Confession and Repentance) 99

Remove the flood of wicked thoughts · Pluck us out of the pit · How have I taken your name in vain? · Set me apart, Lord · We are so sleepy · From heaviness to joy · A prayer of remorse for the nation · I need your remedy · Will you forget me forever? · Let me dwell in your mansion, Lord · You did not die just for all the little sins · I fly to you for refuge · I am a fruitless tree, but... · Still we struggle with our pride · Save me from the flood · You pronounce me "not guilty" · We have wandered, but you will raise us up · We remain here, for now · May we trade in our righteousness? · I trade my heart of stone for a new one · Help us to mourn

You Reach Us in Your Mercy (Prayers of Hope) 123

Please adopt me · We are your children ... and your spouse · Be close, Lord, in our marriage and home · There but for your grace · I am putting on new robes · A prayer for faith, forever! · A prayer at baptism for the gift of faith · Shake us to life · I crave the sunlight of your Spirit · Would you let us know you more each day? · Help us never to claim our own righteousness · A prayer for true humility ·

Heal the pride in our hearts · We will wait for true happiness · Help us to appreciate your gifts, without envy · May we mourn that our sins pierced your side · Help me to pass along your gifts · Keep us humble · Help us to keep the right treasure · A prayer for compassion on my way to work · Help us to look first to our neighbors · Let me fly to you in prayer · I do not measure up · From passion comes life and glory · I welcome the new me · There is no other hope · Keep us from hardening our hearts · Grant me the power to do · We did not deserve this · There is only one cure · We are your flock—I come to you · Mercy upon mercy flows from you · I pray to you in my troubles · We want to be that peculiar people · We turn from the world · turn us to you · Let us remember you and put aside the world · Clothe us for the wedding · Help us to nail our sins on your cross

SHOW US THE WAY
(PRAYERS FOR WISDOM AND GUIDANCE) 159

Help us to listen! · Open our eyes to the light · Give us faithful fishers · A prayer before I dare to preach · Bring us good judges · Help us find our true north · As we make our way through darkness · A prayer for spiritual light · The portrait became clear in your word · Spirit, lead us · Help me to keep learning · Show me your way, the only way · A prayer for finding that right someone · You are the only one who knows the way · In search of purpose · Deliver us from fake religion · May I truly understand your word · Help us to know (and live) the difference · May we see how far we fell · Teach us your mysteries · Before I preach, a word of prayer · Help us to learn our lessons well · May your word penetrate our hearts · Light up my mind · We are going to study scripture—help us! · I seek you, Lord, before opening my Bible · Before we study your word, a prayer · Grant me your wisdom · If you hear me, you hear the Son

Help Us to Follow You
(Prayers for Obedience)

183

Give us a godly love · Help us to seek justice in our daily work · Help us to truly love those who do not love us · Help us always to respect our neighbor · Help us to walk as you did · Let us work without a care · Help me to truly follow you · Recover me and make me more like you · Help us to know the same joy that we share · Give us the right words, at the right time · Keep the spotlight off us, Lord · We are pilgrims—keep us on the road · You invite us to stay on the path · We are so timid, too timid · Give us courage to stand · Bless your word unto us · Help me to speak of you—from my heart

Remember Your Sheep
(Prayers for the Church)

199

Let me praise you forever and ever · We remember our spiritual heritage · Keep us in the way of truth · I believe in the church · You will gather us! · A lament for holy living in the church · Help me to serve you in my work and beyond · The way is so very narrow · We pray for church leadership · Purify your church, Lord · For all who would be pastors · Grant us unity in the battle · Help your church through this storm · Let your shepherds be clothed with righteousness · Protect and defend your church, Lord! · Protect your church and keep us from falling · Preserve the church and give us peace · You alone are the hope of the world · As we worship together, we pray · Defend your church, Lord · Guide, govern, and prosper us

Teach Us to Pray and Share
(The Lord's Prayer and Communion)   223

May I not covet—not even their dog · Write your laws on my heart · Teach us to keep your name holy · May your kingdom come in our lives · We remember your mercy (before communion) · Your will be done · Give us our true daily bread · Lend us your grace (after communion) · Forgive us our debts, and remove our heavy burdens · Give us our daily bread—but nothing more · Lead us not into temptations—all of them · You have nourished and fed our souls (after communion) · Deliver us from evil, amen · A prayer together as we share communion · The Lord's Prayer, expanded · Increase the fervor of our love (after communion) · "Our Father," not "my Father" · So your name may be glorified, not us

Watch Over Us Every Day
(Prayers for Protection)   247

You are my only hope · Do not let me be tempted beyond what I can bear · Keep me from a flimsy gospel · Guard us all our days · Let the trumpet of your holy gospel sound! · Help! The enemy hates us! · We pray for persecuted believers · Protect your truth in this troubled time · A quiet life in the midst of persecution · Keep us until that day · Protect me from your enemies, according to Psalm 139 · If you appear, you will scare the devil away · We stand against the devil—but only in your power · Before a journey · From an expecting mother to the author of life · Grant us patience in trouble · You are the way · A prayer for Christian unity, according to Psalm 68 · I call for help · Look down on us and this small portion of earth

On the Way to Your Peace
(Prayers of Anticipation) 267

Thank you for my home, my refuge · Help us fight to the end · A prayer for the prodigal's brother · Bring down what opposes your word · Give us strength to overcome · We lift up those who need to know you · Help us to never presume on our own strength · Do not let those who despise you be cursed · May I long for heaven, my home · Grant us peace as we return home · Fix our thoughts on heaven · Give us a sample of heaven's sweetness · Conserve me and keep me as your child · Keep our eyes open, looking for your return · We live until that day · When may I come to be with you? · We look to the resurrection day · We look forward to glory · Help us look past the temporary to the eternal

Give Us Grace This Day
(Morning Prayers) 287

A morning prayer for peace · Teach me this day to do your will · A short prayer for when I rise · Give us today what we need to serve you · A prayer for Sunday morning · I bless you early in the morning · A prayer as I wake · Preserve my body and soul today · Awaken me, body and soul · Clothe me with yourself · I follow you as the sun rises · Restore us again to your favor · Let me be dressed in your power · I wake today to praise you

You Give, and We Gather
(Mealtime Prayers) 303

A prayer before meals · A short prayer before a meal · A short prayer after a meal · Your physical food sustains, and so does the eternal · Help us to share your daily gift of food · Waiting on the food that will last forever · The blessing of your presence at a meal

Be Our Watchman in the Night (Evening Prayers)

309

In the evening of life I lift my hands to you · Defend me from the perils and dangers of this night · A prayer as I fall asleep · Abide with us as evening falls · Preserve me as I sleep · Drive away the dimness · Keep us from falling asleep in sin · Let my heart never stop watching you · Keep my tongue and let me trust in you alone

Notes	319
Biographies and Sources	321
Index of Authors and Sources	349

Introduction

Did men and women of the Reformation century—generally speaking, the 1500s—realize how truly historic was their time? Did they feel the spiritual earthquake? We read of them in our history books and wonder.

Before the Reformation took hold, many of these people had sheltered behind the thick stone walls of candle-lit monasteries and convents scattered throughout Europe. Had they chosen differently, perhaps they could have remained there to live out quiet, everyday lives.

But of course they did not. And what began as a trickle with academic debate questions posted on the door of Luther's Wittenberg church would burst forth within a few short months into a massive flood of change. Those monks, nuns, and ordinary believers could not escape the irresistible currents of "sola Scriptura" (scripture alone) and "sola fide" (faith alone), nor would they avoid the sometimes violent or even life-threatening consequences of stepping into the rushing Reformation river.

Five hundred years later, we do our best to trace the course of church history, knowing how easy it is to overlook the eddies and cross-currents. Because along with many inspiring examples, this stream also carried much dissent: German-speaking Lutherans who strongly disagreed with French-speaking Calvinists, or Dutch Anabaptists who attracted scorn as they prayed for peace. Reformers would argue readily and passionately among themselves about modes of baptism, icons in the sanctuary, the role of church authority, civic involvement, and the presence of Christ in communion … The list goes on.

Then there was England, which lagged only a few years behind the first waves of Reformation change in German- and French-speaking Europe. Encouraged by recognition of Protestant principles under Henry VIII and Edward VI, enthusiastic English Reformers found themselves high and dry when Queen Mary I abruptly reversed course and reasserted Catholic primacy. Though England would once again embrace the Anglican church after Mary's death, many outspoken Protestants meanwhile had to flee for their lives to the continent. Not everyone made it.

Still, the flood of this Reformation current would prove unstoppable. God would use imperfect, often headstrong believers to renew the church throughout continental Europe, England, and the New World—despite disagreements, false starts, misunderstandings, and heated debates.

So yes, the church grew in a fresh, new way through all that and more. After all, these were people of prayer. And fortunately for those of us living so far downstream in the timeline, many men (and several women) left behind *written* prayers—prayers that would help us understand the essence of what truly mattered to them. Today these prayers provide some of the best and deepest insights into the Reformers' vibrant, courageous faith.

That's not to say the prayers have always been easy to locate. Some were buried in sermons, others sprinkled without warning into commentary or tied to the conclusion of a lecture. It's safe to assume their writers had little or no intention of sharing such prayers beyond their immediate contemporary audience.

Yet here they are once more. And the remarkable thing is how fresh and applicable those five-hundred-year-old prayers remain today, after just a bit of editing and updated language. As the writer of Ecclesiastes so aptly reminded us, "What has been is what will be" (Ecclesiastes 1:9, ESV).

Ultimately, the prayers included in this collection shine light on some of the most heartfelt facets of the Reformers' faith. In one prayer, for instance, Heinrich Bullinger told God, "You are the source of continual running fountains of all good graces—they never run dry."[1] Myles Coverdale begged the Lord in his prayers to "kindle our cold hearts with the fire of faith."[2] And the incandescent Martin Luther asked God to "make us feel and taste the sweetness of childlike trust, so that we may with joy call you Father."[3]

Mercy. Fountains of good graces. The sweetness of childlike trust. If the Reformers were courageous spiritual warriors who stood tall in the battlefield of faith (come what may!), then in their quieter moments they also eagerly sought the simple embrace of their loving heavenly Father. They revealed a more vulnerable, needy side in these unguarded prayers. In this we, too, can take comfort.

So even if these men and women did appear somewhat stern and unyielding in historical accounts (and such qualities are relatively easy for historians to portray from a safe distance of five hundred years), God has a way of tenderizing hearts in prayer. The child in all of us makes an appearance when we're on our knees.

With that in mind, what is the ultimate value of this collection for us today?

On one level, we gain insight into the passions and needs of fellow believers during a remarkable period of church history. That's well enough. More than that, however, through these prayers we may also join them in a never-ending chorus. Keep in mind how the beloved wife of John Calvin, Idelette, cried out to the Lord on her deathbed in 1549: "O glorious resurrection! In you have all the faithful trusted during so many past ages, and none of them have trusted in vain. I also will hope."[4]

Like Idelette, we too can hope. And this hope rises as a recurring theme throughout these prayers. Do you hear it? As we pray, we discover daily hope, as well as hope in the midst of God's community. I also will hope! We also will hope!

May we then hope *together* as we pray the words of these Reformation prayers, and may we know the freedom to unashamedly reclaim these prayers as our own, in our own times of prayer.

— *Robert Elmer*

LIST OF AUTHORS

ANABAPTIST

GEORG BLAUROCK (1491–1529)

ANNA OF FREIBERG (DIED 1529)

BALTHASAR HUBMAIER (1480–1528)

MENNO SIMONS (1496–1561)

DENMARK

NIELS HEMMINGSEN (1513–1600)

HANS TAUSEN (1494–1561)

ENGLAND/SCOTLAND

HENRY AIRAY (1560–1616)

LANCELOT ANDREWES (1555–1626)

THOMAS BECON (1511–1567)

JOHN BRADFORD (1510–1555)

MYLES COVERDALE (1488–1569)

THOMAS CRANMER (1489–1556)

JOHN DOWNAME (1571–1652)

LADY JANE GREY (1537–1554)

JOHN KNOX (1514–1572)

PRAYER BOOK OF 1578 (1578)

PRIMER OF 1559 (1559)

ROBERT ROLLOCK (1555–1599)

WILLIAM TYNDALE (1495–1536)

JOHN WYCLIFFE (1331–1384)

FRANCE

MARGUERITE DE NAVARRE (1491–1549)

GERMANY

MARTIN BUCER (1491–1551)

ELISABETH CRUCIGER (1500–1535)

JOHANN GERHARD (1582–1637)

MARTIN LUTHER (1483–1546)

PHILIP MELANCHTHON (1497–1560)

NICHOLAUS SELNECKER (1532–1592)

ZACHARIUS URSINUS (1534–1583)

ITALY

    PETER MARTYR VERMIGLI (1499–1562)

SWITZERLAND (GENEVA)

    THEODORE BEZA (1519–1605)

    JOHN CALVIN (1509–1564)

    WILLIAM FAREL (1489–1565)

SWITZERLAND (ZÜRICH)

    HEINRICH BULLINGER (1504–1575)

    HULDRYCH ZWINGLI (1484–1531)

THE PRAYERS

ALIVE IN YOUR GRACE

(PRAYERS OF PRAISE)

LOOKING TO THE SKY, WE PRAISE YOUR NAME

You made heaven and earth for our sake, mighty God. You made the sun and moon for our use, as though they were our servants.

Raise our minds heavenward and upward to think on your true glory, by these your blessings.

May we faithfully worship you alone, surrendering ourselves entirely to you. Even while we enjoy the benefits of all the stars—and also the entire earth—may we know that we are bound to you by so many favors, that we may be more and more roused to do what is just and right.

So we will work to glorify your name on the earth, as we enjoy the blessed glory which comes from Christ our Lord, amen.

—*John Calvin*

JESUS, YOUR NAME IS SWEET

Lord, your name is good! Sweet and glorious, full of health. We desire your name!

Wicked spirits cannot bear you, when they behold Jesus—either in mind, or if they hear the name actually spoken.

I sought to love Jesus, and the more I grew complete in his love, so much the sweeter and savory was his name to me. So the name of Jesus is blessed forever and ever, and so be it. Amen.

—*John Wycliffe*

Teach us in the school of praise

Almighty God, though we see and hear so many testimonies of your glory every day, we can be so blind and shut out all the light by our ingratitude.

Teach us to open our eyes. Yes, open them by your Spirit! Help us to spend time thinking on how many, how great, and how deep are your blessings toward us.

And while you set before us the proof of your eternal divinity, help us to excel in this school of devotion. May we learn to give you all praise, until there is nothing left to do but to glorify you alone. May we all the more grow in our ardent desire to worship you, the more you bend down to us in grace.

May we also devote ourselves to you and grow to care about this one thing: that your glory may remain and shine forth throughout all the world, through Christ our Lord, amen.

—John Calvin

TO THE GOD WHO IS BEYOND COMPREHENDING

Up with our hearts—we lift them up to you, Lord.

It is right, fitting, and due in all things, for all things, at all times, in all places, by all means, in every season, everywhere, every way, to mention you, to worship and praise you, to bless you and sing to you, to give thanks to you, and to confess our sins before you.

You are the maker, nourisher, and preserver. The governor, protector, author, and finisher of all. You are the Lord and father, king and God, the fountain of everlasting life, the treasure of eternal good things.

The heavens sing your praises with the angels and all heavenly powers. They never stop calling out your praise. So we join in from under their feet, weak and unworthy, to cry "holy, holy, holy, Lord God of hosts."

Heaven and earth are full of your glory. We bless you for everything about you that we will never comprehend— for your Godhead, your height, your sovereignty, your almightiness and eternity, and your guidance and care.

You are my strength and my rock, my defense and my savior, my might, my shield, the source of my salvation, and my refuge. Amen.

— Lancelot Andrewes

Your name is great

Lord God Almighty, by your Spirit you have united us into your one body in the unity of the faith. You have commanded your body to give praise and thanks unto you for that bounty and kindness with which you have delivered your only begotten Son, our Lord Jesus Christ, unto death for our sins.

Now grant that we may fulfill this command in faith, never offending or provoking you with false displays. You are the infallible truth.

Grant also that we may live purely—the way we should as your body, your children, and your family. That way, may even unbelievers learn to recognize your name and your glory.

Keep us, Lord, so your name and glory are never tarnished through the depravity of our lives.

We always pray, "Lord, increase our faith. Increase our trust in you, who lives and reigns, world without end."

And we respond as your church: Amen.

— *Huldrych Zwingli*

Joining in the concert of praise

We praise you, Lord. Holy one, you are worthy to receive glory, honor, and power. All flesh will come to you—you hear our prayers. I come, too.

My sins have overwhelmed me. But show mercy, so I may come and give thanks and bless you with all the believers for all that you have done. Open my lips, Lord, and my mouth will speak your praise.

My soul praises you, Lord, for the goodness you have done throughout all creation. I praise you for the mercy you have shown me: body, soul, right here and now. I praise you for the mercy you have shown all humanity. For health and safety, for a quiet life.

You have not cut off my life; you have granted me breath until this hour, from childhood even until now. You have rescued me from dangers, sickness, poverty, bondage, public shame, and evil. You did not give me up to die in my sins as you waited for me to turn to you in faith. You let me turn to my heart and remember—with a measure of shame and grief, even horror at my past sins.

Give me now a larger and fuller vision of my need, Lord. You have granted me the good hope that you will melt away those sins as I repent, by your power. I call to mind your benefits, and even for those I have not known about, I confess and give thanks to you. I bless and praise you every day.

And I pray with my whole soul, with my whole mind: Glory be to you, Lord, glory to you and to your all-holy name.

Glory to you for your divine perfection. Glory to you for your incomprehensible and incomparable goodness. Glory to you for your mercy toward sinners and unworthy people— and toward me—of all sinners the most unworthy by far.

For all this and for the rest, Lord, I give you glory and praise, blessing and thanks. I join my voice in the concert of mortals and angels, of all your saints in heaven, and all your creatures in heaven or on earth—though I remain beneath their feet, an unworthy and wretched sinner.

I am your humble creature, now, in this day and hour, and every day until my last breath, and until the end of the world, forever and ever, amen.

— *Lancelot Andrewes*

I PASS ALL THINGS TO YOU

As I walk among the snares of this world, Lord Jesus, I pray that you would defend me from all the plagues and subtle dangers. Grant that I would contend as I should with all things that happen—by setting my eyes only on you, moving ahead unhindered in your way, and passing along all things to you.

"Make me to know your ways, O Lord; teach me your paths" (Psalm 25:4).

Amen.

— *John Bradford*

No sweeter name

What can be sweeter than the name of Jesus!

O blessed Jesus, would you indeed be a Jesus to me. For your holy name's sake have compassion on me!

My life condemns me, but the name of Jesus will save me. For your name's sake deal with me according to your name. And since you are a true and great savior, you will surely treat those who are real and great sinners with mercy.

Have mercy on me, blessed Jesus, in the day of mercy, so as not to condemn me in the day of judgment. If you will receive me in the arms of your compassion, you will not be reduced on my account. If you will allow me crumbs of your goodness, you will not be made poorer. You were born for me (Isaiah 9:6) and for me you are Jesus.

How sweet and delightful is the name of Jesus! For what is Jesus but Savior? And what real harm can happen to the saved? What beyond salvation can we seek or expect?

Receive me, O Lord Jesus, as your child, so that as your child I may praise your holy and saving name. If I have lost my original innocence through my sin, have I deprived you of your mercy? Even if I have miserably destroyed and condemned myself, can you not still compassionately save me?

Do not so regard my sins, O Lord, as to forget your own mercy. Do not so weigh and measure my offenses so they outweigh your merit. Do not so consider my evil as to overlook your own good. Do not remember wrath against a culprit, but remember your mercy toward a miserable sinner.

Lord, you have given me a desire for you, so won't you fulfill my longing desire? You who have shown me my unworthiness and just condemnation, will you hide from me your merit and promise of eternal life? My cause must be tried before a heavenly tribunal. But it comforts me that in this court the name of savior has been given you. That blessed name was brought from heaven by the angel (Luke 2:21).

Most merciful Jesus, to whom will you be a Jesus, if not to wretched sinners seeking grace and salvation?

Those who trust in their own righteousness and holiness seek salvation in themselves. But I find in me nothing worthy of eternal life, so I flee to you as my savior. Save me, for I am condemned. Have mercy on me, for I am a sinner. Justify me, for I am unrighteous. Acquit me, for I am accused of sin.

Lord, you are the truth (John 14:6). Your name is holy and true, so let your name be true in respect to me. Be my Jesus and my savior! Be my Jesus in this life; be my Jesus in death. Be my Jesus in the last judgment and in eternal life. And surely you will be, blessed Jesus, because as you are unchangeable in essence so will you be in mercy.

Your name will not be changed, Lord Jesus, on account of one miserable sinner like me. You will not cast out anyone who comes to you. You have given me the desire to come to you, and surely you will receive me when I do come, for your words are Spirit and life (John 6:63). Amen.

— *Johann Gerhard*

LET OUR HEARTS PURSUE YOU, LORD CHRIST

Lord Christ, God's only dear Son, you have sprung from the Father's heart from eternity, as we see in the Scriptures. Morning star, you gleam brighter than all stars in the sky.

You were born of a pure virgin in the fullness of time. Your death has opened for us the gates of heaven and restored life to us.

Lord Christ, let us adore you in love, increasing in the knowledge of you. Despite our earthly weakness, let us serve you in spirit and never cease in faith, that our hearts may taste your sweetness, and ever thirst for you.

You who founded the whole world, and who, in your unbounded power and fatherly might reign over day and night—let our hearts pursue you and let us turn our minds to you, lest we stray.

Lord, kill us with your goodness. Make us alive in your grace. While we still live on this earth, take away our old nature, and replace it with new life. And may our every thought, desire, and feeling cleave to you. Amen.

— *Elisabeth Cruciger*

LIGHT UP MY LIFE, LORD

O Lord, you are the greatest and most true light. This day's light and sun spring from you.

O Light, you illuminate everyone who comes into this world. You know neither evening nor night, but are always midday, clear and fair.

Without you, everything is darkness. Wisdom of the eternal, you make everything brilliant.

Father of mercies, light up my mind, that I may only see those things that please you. Blind me to all else. Help me to always walk in your ways, and grant that nothing else would be light or pleasant to me.

Light up my eyes, lest I sleep the sleep of death, lest my enemy say, "I have prevailed over him" (Psalm 13:3–4).

Amen.

— *John Bradford*

No other name comes close!

O Jesus Christ, Son of God, let us not lack your favor. For what would we deserve if we, the salt, were to lose our flavor?

With an angry flame people try to destroy all traces of your name—but in vain, because your word stands sure forever.

As believers, then, God, we praise you in unity. We praise you that you have spread your word and your work abroad. No human, and no other name can withstand you.

Your word stands sure forever. We sing our glad amen!

— *Balthasar Hubmaier*

We See Your Goodness

(Prayers of Recognition and Thanks)

Holy Spirit, come!

Holy Spirit, you are worthy of all worship. In the almighty Trinity you proceed from the Father and the Son, and you are equal to either of them.

With your holy breath you cleanse our minds. You comfort us in sorrow and cheer us with pure gladness. You lead us into all truth, and you kindle the fire of love in us. You knit us together with the glue of peace, and you enrich us with gifts by which we profess the name of the Lord Jesus—by whose working all things live, and whose delight is to live in our hearts.

I ask now that you would maintain your gifts in me, and increase them daily, so that by your governance the desires of the flesh may die more and more in me, and the desire for the heavenly life would come alive and increase.

Let me pass through the misty desert of this world, with your light leading me on. May I not be defiled by Satan's vices. And may I not be entangled with errors that disagree with your truth—delivered by the true church under your guidance.

You live and reign with the Father and the Son, amen.

— Book of Christian Prayers of 1578

MAY WE NOT MISUSE YOUR GIFTS

Generous giver of all your gifts, you give us all kinds of good things to use. Because you are pure, you give us pure things. Grant us the grace to not misuse your gifts.

Help us not to love the gifts just because you gave them to us. Instead, may we love you because you gave them. They may be necessary for a time until we come to you.

And then help us to use the gifts in a sober, pure, temperate, and holy way—because that is what you are. So we will not turn the gifts (which you have given as a kind of medicine for our bodies) into poison for our souls. But as we use the gifts with thanks, we will find them useful for body and soul.

Amen.

—*John Bradford*

THANK YOU FOR THE BLESSINGS
OF RELATIONSHIPS

Lord, thank you for my parents, my teachers, and for so many others you have placed over me.

I cannot describe all the blessings I have received since I was born. How good you have been to me! In and by these people you have nourished, fed, instructed, corrected, defended, and most graciously kept me. You have engraved on their hearts a desire to care for me, to do me good, and to provide for me.

Be merciful now to my entire family, gracious Lord, as you know they all have need. Strengthen the hearts of all parents and other trusted authority figures, that they may serve faithfully, carefully, and diligently. And help those children they serve to then be able to respond in love, obedience, and thankfulness.

Bless our church and community as places or peace and safety, and send your peace to our homes and families. Finally, write all your laws on our hearts, we pray, that we may keep them. Amen.

— *John Bradford*

YOU ONLY GIVE US WHAT WE NEED

We give you thanks, Lord God, for all the benefits we continue to receive from your generous hand. You not only give us what we need in this life, but in your free mercy you have fashioned us anew into an assured hope of a far better life—declared to us in the gospel.

So we humbly ask, heavenly Father, do not let our affections be so entangled or rooted in these earthly things that will not last. Instead may we always have our minds directed to you on high, always watching for the coming of our Lord and Savior, when he will appear for our full redemption. To whom, with you and the Holy Spirit, be all honor and glory, forever and ever. So be it.

—John Knox

MAY YOUR SPIRIT BE PRESENT
AS WE MEET

I appeal to you, Almighty God, that your Spirit, which you have promised us, and which you have never denied to those who are rightly gathered together in your name, may be present both with me speaking, and with those hearing.

Take away the mist of our ignorance, and cleanse our minds from the corruption of sin, so that none of us will have need to repent of our efforts.

Amen.

— Theodore Beza

THANK YOU FOR YOUR GIFTS OF GRACE

O Lord, my Lord, I give you thanks for my being, for my life. Thank you for nurturing, protecting, and guiding me. Thank you for teaching me, for freedom, and for faith.

For your gifts of grace, for my redemption and regeneration. For calling me and recalling me—yes, for recalling me again and again. For your patience and longsuffering to me, many times, many years, up to this day.

For success you've granted me, and all the good things you've done for me. For things present, for your promise, and for hope of the enjoyment of good things to come.

For my family and teachers, and for those who have blessed me. (I will never forget them.) For brothers and sisters in faith, thoughtful listeners, true friends, faithful co-workers.

For all who have helped me by what they have written and preached, for conversations, prayers, examples, rebukes, injuries. ... For all these, and all others which I know, which I know not, for things open and hidden, for that which I've remembered and forgotten, or done when I wished—and even when I did not wish, I bless you, Lord. And I will bless. I give thanks to you, Lord. And I will give thanks, all the days of my life.

Who am I that you should look on someone like me? How could I ever pay you back, Lord, for all the benefits you have given me? What thanks could I ever give you for sparing me, and bearing with me?

Holy, holy, holy! You are worthy, our Lord and God, the Holy One, to receive glory and honor and power. For you have made all things. And for your pleasure they are—and were—created.

Amen.

— Lancelot Andrewes

HELP ME PRAY WITH MY WHOLE HEART

Good Father, give me plentifully of your Spirit, which you have promised to "pour out … on all flesh" (Joel 2:28), so I may with your saints talk with you night and day.

Oh that your Spirit might so affect me, that with heart and voice I would altogether and in faith pray to you! Give me a true love of others while always preferring your glory above all things.

Help me that I might love you with all my heart, come to you with all my needs, and always by prayer pour out my heart before you. For the sake of your beloved Son, Jesus Christ our Lord, amen.

—John Bradford

THANKSGIVING IN A TIME
OF PERSECUTION

Gracious God, you seek every means to bring your children into the feeling and sure sense of your mercy. When prosperity does not work, you send adversity, and you graciously correct those people who will live with you forever.

We give you our humble praise and thanks, dear Father, that you consider us worthy of your correction. You work in us that which we neglected when we had prosperity and liberty. And you might justifiably have given us over to our grievous sins, destroying us in body and soul.

But your goodness to us in Christ is such that you seem to forget all our offenses. Now you allow us to suffer this cross, now laid on us for the sake of your truth and your gospel. We are your witnesses now, along with the prophets, apostles, martyrs, and those who confess your name. We are your witnesses even with your dearly beloved Son, and you are beginning to fashion us to be more like him, in his glory.

Who are we, good God, that you should show us this great mercy? Forgive us our unthankfulness and sins, and give us your Holy Spirit now to cry "Abba, Father!" in our hearts. Assure us of our eternal election in Christ, and reveal more and more of your truth to us. Confirm, strengthen, and establish us—so we may live and die as vessels of your mercy, to your glory and for the good of the church.

Spread over us the Spirit of your wisdom, so that with a good conscience we may always answer the enemies of your cause, turning them to confusion or conversion. With the unspeakable consolation of Jesus Christ, keep us and give us patience. Deliver us or ease our misery only in line with your good pleasure and merciful will.

Grant this, dear Father, not only to us in this place, but also to all others who are afflicted in other places—for your name's sake, and through the death and merits of Jesus Christ our Lord. Amen.

— John Bradford

I THANK YOU, MORE THAN I CAN SAY

Eternal God and merciful Father, I give you thanks by your well-beloved Son, our only mediator, Lord, and Savior Jesus Christ, for all your gifts and benefits—physical gifts as well as spiritual, temporal as well as eternal.

Each gift is more and far greater than my mind can understand or my words express. Amen.

— Niels Hemmingsen

YOU CROWN THE YEAR
WITH YOUR GOODNESS

Hosanna upon the earth. Lord, remember to crown the year with your goodness—for the eyes of all wait upon you, and you give them their food in due season.

You open your hand, and fill all living things with your plenty. Grant us the blessings of heaven and of the dew from above, blessings of fountains from the deep, of the sun and moon, the ancient mountains and hills, the precious things of the earth and of its fullness.

Grant us good seasons, wholesome weather, full crops and plenteous fruits, health of body, peaceful times, good government and good laws, wise leaders, equal judgments, loyal obedience, and vigorous justice.

May we also enjoy growing families and happiness as we train and nurture our children. May our sons and daughters grow up healthy. And in our communities may there be no decay, no falling into captivity, and no complaining in our streets. Amen.

— *Lancelot Andrewes*

THANKS FOR THE GIFT OF BAPTISM

O dear Lord, eternal God and Heavenly Father, I thank you from my heart for your unspeakably great grace and mercy. Thank you for so graciously allowing me, a poor, unworthy sinner, to come to this holy baptism, and that you have given me knowledge and a right understanding of your divine word and fatherly will.

Gracious Father, I pray that you would give me your Holy Spirit to live in my heart, to guide and encourage me to live according to your holy word, that I would never despise or neglect to listen and learn. But lay it on my inner heart so that it may create good fruit in me, and that by your word in me may be born a Christlikeness and holiness, and that I may live all my days to please you and follow your will.

By your Son my dear Lord Jesus Christ, who with you and the Holy Spirit lives and reigns, amen.

— *Hans Tausen*

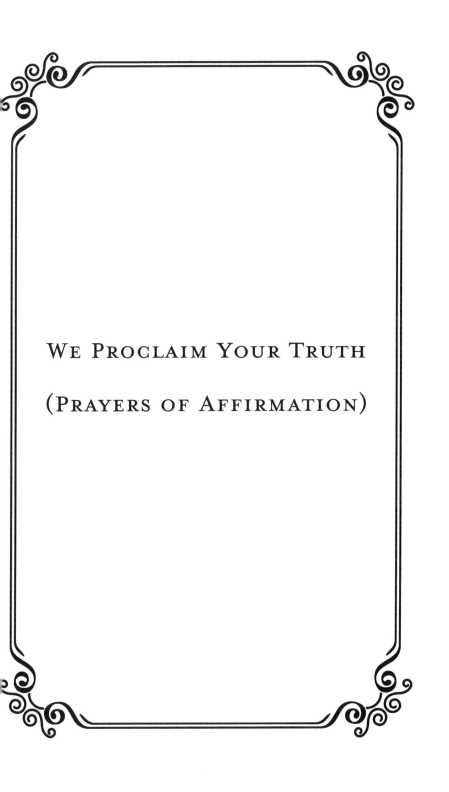

We Proclaim Your Truth

(Prayers of Affirmation)

I BELIEVE!

Lord, I believe in you—Father, Word, Spirit, one God.

I believe all things were created by your fatherly love and power.

I believe that by your goodness and love for humanity all things have been gathered together in your Word—who for us and for our salvation was made flesh, was conceived and born, suffered and was crucified, died and was buried, descended and rose again, ascended and sat down, will return and will repay.

I believe that by the illumination and working of your Holy Spirit we have been called out of the world as a distinct people—we who believe in truth and holiness. We have a part in the communion of saints and forgiveness of sins, and we await the resurrection of our bodies and life everlasting in the world to come.

I believe this most holy faith which was once delivered to the saints. I believe, O Lord; help my unbelief! Increase my smallness of faith. Help me to love the Father for his fatherly love, to reverence the Almighty for his power as a faithful Creator, and to commit my soul to him.

Let me experience salvation from Jesus, anointing from Christ, and adoption from the only-begotten Son.

Let me serve the Lord ... for his conception, in faith. For his birth, in humility. For his sufferings, in patience and hatred of sin. For his cross, to crucify occasions of sin. For his death, to mortify the flesh. For his burial, to bury evil thoughts through good works. For his descent, to consider the reality of hades. For his resurrection, to see newness of life. For his ascension, to set my mind on things above. For his sitting on high, to recognize the good things at his right hand. For his return, to stand in awe of his second coming. For his judgment, to judge myself before I am judged.

Grant me the breath of saving grace from the Spirit. Show me my calling, holiness, and portion in the church. And let me share there the fellowship of worship, prayers, fastings, trials, watchings, tears, suffering, remission of sins, and that confident hope of resurrection and translation to eternal life, amen.

— *Lancelot Andrewes*

I BELIEVE IN REPENTANCE

Lord, I believe and confess that your Christian Church has received keys. We have a command and power from you, Christ Jesus, to open the gates of heaven for sinners as often as they repent and are sorry for their sin, receiving them again into the holy assembly of believers in Christ, like the lost son.

But when sinners will not abstain from sin—even after the threefold brotherly reproof—I firmly believe that this church also has power to exclude and to consider them as we would a heathen and outsider.

Amen.

— *Balthasar Hubmaier*

I LIFT UP MY SOUL

To you, O Lord, I lift up my soul. In you, my God, I trust. Do not let me be put to shame.

Lord of heaven and earth, I call you Lord, though I am not worthy to be called your servant. I do not doubt your grace, for I find in the word of your truth that you are a bountiful, rich Lord to all who call upon you.

So I call unto you, Lord. Hear me!

With full confidence and assurance, I lift up my soul and my heart to you alone. You are my Lord and Father, our Redeemer.

I trust in you, for I truly know that you are a faithful God to all who trust in you. If I am in darkness, you are my light. If I am in prison, you are with me. If I am abandoned, you are my comfort. In death, you are my life. If others curse me, you bless. If others give me grief, you comfort. If they slay me, you will raise me up. And if I walk in the dark valley, you will always be with me.

It is right, O Lord, that I lift up my grieved soul to you. I trust in your promise, and I am not ashamed. Amen.

— *Menno Simons*

Keep me in faith until my end

Holy, mighty, immortal God, I believe what I confessed with my heart and mouth when I was baptized.

Faithfully, graciously, keep me in that belief until my end, I pray. Even if I am driven from it by human fear or terror, by tyranny, pain, or violence, yet I cry to you, O my merciful Father:

Raise me up again by the grace of your Holy Spirit. Do not let me depart in death without this faith.

This I pray you from the bottom of my heart, through Jesus Christ, your best-beloved Son, our Lord and Savior. For I hope in you, Father. Let me not be put to shame in eternity.

Amen.

— Balthasar Hubmaier

I BELIEVE THE HOLY SPIRIT IS IN ME

My Lord Jesus Christ, I believe and confess that you were conceived by the Holy Spirit, without any human seed, and born from Mary, the pure virgin.

I believe that you bring again to me (and to all who believe!) the grace of the Holy Spirit, obtained from your Heavenly Father. This grace was withdrawn from me by reason of my sin.

I believe and trust that the Holy Spirit has come in me, and the power of the most high God has, as with Mary, overshadowed my soul. So I may conceive the new person—and so in your living, indestructible word and in the Spirit, I may be born again and see the kingdom of God.

For you, Son of the living God, did become a man, in order that through you we might become children of God.

Amen.

— *Balthasar Hubmaier*

I BELIEVE ALL IS NOT LOST

I believe in you, God the Father Almighty, maker of heaven and earth.

You are my most precious Lord and merciful Father. For my sake you have created heaven and earth and all that is in them. And now in your fatherly grace you have made me, your beloved child, a ruler and heir—to remain here and to live eternally.

I confess that by the disobedience of Adam, we humans lost this grace-filled sonship. We lost this honor and heirship. Even so, I set all my comfort, hope, and trust in you as my most gracious Father. And I know surely and certainly that this fall will not bring me condemnation.

Amen.

— *Balthasar Hubmaier*

I believe in Jesus Christ

Father, I believe in Jesus Christ, your only begotten Son, our Lord. And I believe that he for my sake has redeemed me before you for the fall. I believe he made peace between you and me, a poor sinner. I believe that by his obedience he obtained again for me the heirship that was lost.

I see in his sent holy word that Christ has again given me power to become your child in faith. I hope in him and trust him wholly. He will not let the saving and comforting name of Jesus be lost on me, a miserable sinner.

For I believe he is Christ—true God and man. He will redeem me from all my sins!

Amen.

— *Balthasar Hubmaier*

I WOULD RATHER BE IN TROUBLE
THAN WITHOUT YOU

Lord, since you have promised to be with me in my afflictions, let me ever be afflicted rather than at any time be without you.

It is better for me to embrace you in times of trouble, and to have you with me in the fiery furnace of affliction, than enjoy all worldly prosperity and to be without your company.

It is better for me to be in trouble while you are with me than to reign and revel, feast and flourish in worldly pomp—and be without you.

It is a far greater good to embrace you in tribulation and to enjoy your company in the fire of affliction than to be in heaven itself, deprived of your presence.

Amen.

—John Downame

I BELIEVE YOU RANSOMED ME
BY YOUR CROSS

Lord, I believe and confess that you suffered under Pontius Pilate, and that you were crucified, dead and buried. It was all because of my sins. You redeemed and ransomed me from an eternal cross, from the pain, suffering, and death. And you did it by your own cross, suffering, anguish, pain, and bitter death—as well as by the pouring out of your blood.

In this we poor humans recognize your greatest and highest love to us. For you have changed for us your heavy cross into a light yoke. You have turned your bitter sufferings into perpetual joys. And you have turned your death in the midst of anger... into eternal life.

So I will praise and thank you, my gracious Lord Jesus Christ, forever and ever.

Amen.

— *Balthasar Hubmaier*

I believe in eternal life

Lord, I believe and confess an eternal life which you, my Lord and God, will give to your faithful and elect after this suffering life.

I believe you will bless us with a sure, clear, and joyous view of your divine appearance. You will satisfy us in all our desires with eternal rest, eternal peace, and eternal salvation. We will be unable to imagine or express here on earth that kind of joy, delight, and bliss.

For no eye has seen, no ear has heard, and no heart has known what God has prepared for those who love him.

Amen.

— *Balthasar Hubmaier*

I am in trouble—and I trust in you

Do not let my enemies gloat over me. Surely none who wait for you will be put to shame.

Lord of hosts, Lord of lords, my flesh is weak and my misery great. Even so, I do not fear my enemies. I only fear that I would deny your name and depart from your truth. Then they would rejoice at my weakness and say, "Where is your God now? Where is your Christ?"

Preserve me and keep me, Lord. My enemies are strong and many. Satan chases me like a roaring lion, seeking to devour me. The bloodthirsty, revengeful world wants my life; they also hate, persecute, burn, and murder those who seek your praise.

I do not know which way to turn. Misery, fear, and dread are on every side. Strife inside, persecution outside.

Abraham and Jacob, Joseph and Moses, David in the mountains, Hezekiah in Jerusalem, the young men in the fiery furnace, Daniel in the lion's den … they all trusted in you, and were not ashamed. So I lift my eyes to you, and depend only on your grace and mercy, amen.

— *Menno Simons*

I BELIEVE YOU HEAR FROM HEAVEN

I believe and confess, my Lord Jesus Christ, that you ascended to heaven and sat down at the right hand of your Heavenly Father after those forty days when you walked on the earth as a testimony of your joyous resurrection. You ascended to the same power, glory, and praise with the Father, who has given to you all power over all his possessions, in heaven and on earth.

And there you sit, mighty and strong, to help all believers who put their trust, comfort, and hope in you, and who cry to you in all their needs.

You also call all those who are burdened to come to you, and you will give them rest. We can pray to you from wherever we are. You are not confined to a particular ceremony, for you are found sitting at the right hand of your Heavenly Father, as Stephen saw you and prayed to you.

It is also futile to seek another advocate. You are and will be the only one.

Amen.

— *Balthasar Hubmaier*

Plant the seed that brings lifetime fruit

Almighty God, since you are pleased to invite us to yourself, and you have set apart your word for our salvation, help us to obey you willingly—from the heart.

May we become so teachable that what you designed for our salvation may not return to condemn us. And may the indestructible seed by which you regenerate us to know that hope for heaven drive its roots into our hearts and bear fruit.

May your name be glorified! Plant us in the courts of your house so that we grow and flourish. And may that fruit appear throughout our entire life, until we at last come to enjoy that blessed life that is prepared for us in heaven, through Christ our Lord, amen.

— John Calvin

I believe you are coming again

I believe and confess that you will come to judge the living and the dead on the day of the last judgment, which will be to all godly believers a specially longed-for and joyous day.

Because then we will see our God and Savior face to face, in your great glory and majesty coming in the clouds of heaven. Then will be ended our fleshly, sinful, and godless life.

O my Lord Jesus Christ, shorten the days and come down to us! Yet give us grace and strength to direct our lives in the meantime so we may be worthy to hear then with joy your gracious and sweet voice, when you will say,

"Come, you who are blessed by my Father, inherit the kingdom prepared for you from the foundation of the world. For I was hungry and you gave me food, I was thirsty and you gave me drink, I was a stranger and you welcomed me, I was naked and you clothed me, I was sick and you visited me, I was in prison and you came to me… Truly, I say to you, as you did it to one of the least of these my brothers, you did it to me" (Matthew 25:34b–36, 40b ESV).

Amen.

— *Balthasar Hubmaier*

I believe in the resurrection

Lord, I believe and confess a resurrection of the flesh, even the body with which I am now surrounded.

And though my worldly honor, goods, body, and life be taken from me, yet will I, at the day of the joyous resurrection of my flesh, first truly receive the true honor before God—goods that never pass away, a body that will never suffer, and eternal life.

O my mediator, Lord Jesus Christ, strengthen and hold me in your faith!

Amen.

— *Balthasar Hubmaier*

I believe in the Holy Spirit

I believe in the Holy Spirit, proceeding from the Father and the Son, and yet with the Father and Son is the only and true God.

The Spirit sanctifies all things, and without him nothing is holy. I fully trust that he will teach me all truth, increase my faith, and kindle the fire of love in my heart by his holy inspiration—truly kindle it that it may burn in true, honest, and Christian love to you and my neighbor.

For that I pray to you from the heart, my God, my Lord, my Comforter.

Amen.

— *Balthasar Hubmaier*

I believe you conquered death

I believe and confess, O Christ—who has mercy on me— that on the third day, you were united together again spirit, soul, and body in the grave.

And like a strong and powerful conqueror of death, hell, and the devil, you rose again from the dead for our sakes, so that all who believe in you should not perish, but in you overcome sin, death, hell, and devils. And in you we obtain eternal life as your co-heir.

Amen.

— *Balthasar Hubmaier*

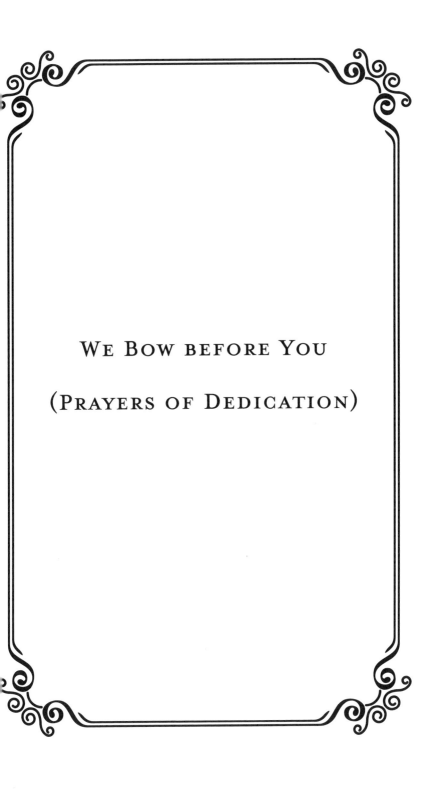

We Bow before You

(Prayers of Dedication)

WE ARE LOADED WITH FAILINGS, BUT YOU INVITE US TO YOURSELF

Almighty God, we are loaded with so many failings, and we provoke you so often—daily, and in uncounted ways. Yet in your fatherly kindness you invite us daily to yourself.

So I pray that we may not become hardened against your godly admonitions, when you urge us to live a holy life. May we not grow callous to your discipline, and never harden ourselves against your holy and life-giving advice. Because if we had heartless, hard attitudes you would have no choice but to put forth your powerful hand against us.

Teach us instead to submit humbly to your word, to repent in time, and so profit as we receive your correction. May our lives testify that our hearts are changed. That way, we avoid the extreme judgment you heap on those who are obstinate.

But since we have experienced your fatherly kindness up to now, so may we experience the same in the future, and thus become more and more accustomed to wearing your yoke. Help us to open a way for your fatherly goodness, so you may deal kindly with us until we finish our battles.

And as we encourage each other and unite in obeying your word, may we glorify your name through Christ Jesus our Lord, amen.

—John Calvin

Keep us working for your glory until the end

Lord Jesus, direct all our work in whatever direction you please. Illuminate and purify our minds and thoughts. Teach us how to humbly begin, diligently do, and blessedly end all our projects—to the praise and honor of your holy name. Help us to follow in your footsteps daily.

Give us grace to labor faithfully in the vineyard of the Lord. Grant that heat or hard work do not get the best of us. Help us to steadfastly endure in the school of heavenly exercise, until we reach our end. And when that end draws close, may we then depart in your mercy and grace to receive the joy of paradise. Through your mercy, after many battles and striving, may we say in the last hour of our life: It is all finished.

May you be the final occasion of our life, and of all our doing. So it will follow that you will also be our eternal reward, our joy, and our salvation. Father, we commit our spirit into your hand. You have redeemed us, God of truth. Let these be our last words. Amen.

— *Myles Coverdale*

The world's disapproval does not matter

Lord, by nature we do not willingly submit to the criticism and contempt of the world.

With our hearts lifted up to heaven, Lord, grant that we would not be concerned how the world disapproves of us. May our faith never waver or fold, even if worldly people ridicule us while we serve you under the cross.

Help us to wait patiently until Christ finally appears in the splendor of his priesthood and kingdom.

Meanwhile, may we think on the excellent gifts you have given the church. May we be encouraged to connect with the few and despised believers who follow your word in faith and sincerity. Help us to disregard the world's arrogance, never doubting that as we remain grounded in the pure gospel, you will raise us up to the place where we will enjoy the blessing your only begotten Son has purchased for us with his own blood. Amen.

— *John Calvin*

We want less of us, more of you

Set apart and dedicate our hearts, Lord, with the touch of your Holy Spirit, so we may worship you in spirit and in truth, and so we may rejoice in your Son Christ Jesus our salvation. Teach us to renounce all confidence in anything that does not include him!

Purge us daily more and more from all overdone affections, and from all those unbridled desires which may draw us away from you or hinder us from serving you.

Renew in us a right spirit, so we may worship you—not in a comfortable way that we dream up on our own, but in spirit and in truth, according to your holy word.

Set us apart and make us holy through your Holy Spirit, so that as we completely abandon all worldly confidence, we may wholly and only rejoice in Christ Jesus forever and ever, amen.

— Henry Airay

GIVE US A SPIRIT TO WEAR YOUR YOKE

Almighty God, when you delivered us from the tyranny of Satan, you placed your yoke on our necks.

Now would you grant us a docile, meek, and obedient spirit—so that we might willingly submit ourselves to you through the whole course of our life?

Please do this so that you may gather from us the fruit of your redemption, and so we may renounce sin and devote ourselves to your service—as servants of righteousness.

Then, having finished the course of our warfare, we will be gathered into that blessed rest which has been obtained for us by the blood of your only-begotten Son. Amen.

— John Calvin

HELP US STAY PURE AS HUSBAND AND WIFE

Gracious good Lord, help me and my spouse to live a relationship that reflects your holiness. Grant that we may keep the vessels of our lives pure and undefiled, following your way.

I ask the same for other married couples. And for those who are unmarried, likewise: that they may live pure and chaste lives, free from coarseness and indecency, undefiled by the world.

And for those singles who do not have the gift of singleness, grant them the kind of husbands or wives with whom they may live holy lives together, to your praise.

Dear Father, give me the gift of sobermindedness and temperance in lifestyle, and grant the same to those whom you would like me to lift up in prayer.

And in contrast to those times past when I used my tongue and my whole self for evil, dear Lord, let me now use them well, in a godly and modest way.

Sanctify and set me apart in body and soul, dear Lord. As you have in your temple, dwell in me now and forevermore. Grant this, I pray, through Christ Jesus, amen.

— *John Bradford*

TRANSFORM MY TONGUE
INTO SOMETHING NEW

Gracious Lord, even as I recognize and acknowledge my unthankfulness, I continue with breathless hypocrisy in all that I say: with frequent lies, vanity, offensiveness, and worldliness. I listen to slander without objecting, and so encourage it to go on. For all this I deserve condemnation.

But good Lord, be merciful to me. I ask for Christ's sake, the one you have ordained to be "the end of the law for righteousness to everyone who believes" (Romans 10:4). And I ask that you would pardon what is past.

In his name therefore, good Lord, I ask that you would give me your holy Spirit to open to me this law and all your other principles. Help me to understand them, so I may love them from my heart, and faithfully give myself to obey them forever.

Grant me your Spirit to sanctify my tongue, that it may be kept from lying, slandering, and all such corruption. Instead may it be continually used in service to you, and for speaking only that which lifts you up in glory and praise, through Jesus Christ our Lord. Amen.

— *John Bradford*

For your sake, Lord, transform me

Begin in me a new and godly life, Lord, devoted to your praise forever. Help me to put off the self and be made a new creature, putting on righteousness, holiness, innocence, and eternal life.

For your poverty's sake, make me rich with your heavenly riches.

For your exile's sake, help me to live this life as an expatriate and make me a citizen of heaven.

For your baptism's sake, grant me the baptism of the Spirit, living as your child and guided by the Spirit forever.

For your fasting and temptation's sake, put to death my affection for living like the world.

For your doctrine's sake, enlighten the eyes of my mind that I may see and follow your path.

For your miracles' sake, heal my wounds, cure my diseases, and restore to me life. Give me inward sight, hearing, and speech. Cast out all evil in me, and come and dwell in me forever.

For your great humility's sake in washing the disciples' feet, wash away from me all my filth of sin and my readiness to do evil. Help me to humble myself to serve others.

For the sake of your sorrow and agony, help me see and hate sin in myself and others. May I not make trivial what was so painful for you to purchase. And may I deny myself, offering myself wholly to you.

For the sake of your love, which made you willing to be taken and bound, loose me from the bonds of all sins, and instead secure me in the loving strings of your will.

Grant, dear Lord, that I may be always ready to suffer gladly all kind of taunts, injuries, contempt, and slander for your name's sake. By your grace, divert my affections, my words, and my deeds to your glory forever.

Amen.

— *John Bradford*

MAY WE EAT FOR YOUR GLORY

As long as our pilgrimage in this world continues, Lord, may we feed only on a diet that is necessary for our bodies—a diet that will not corrupt us. May we also never be led aside from sober-mindedness, but may we learn to use our abundance by instead preferring restraint and self-control in the midst of plenty.

Grant also, Lord, that we may patiently endure want and famine. May we eat and drink with the kind of liberty that will always elevate before us the glory of your name.

Finally, may our careful economy lead us to pursue that fullness by which we will be completely refreshed when we behold your glory in heaven, through Jesus Christ our Lord. Amen.

— *John Calvin*

FILL THIS EMPTY VESSEL

Lord, I pour out my heart before you. See, here is an empty vessel, which greatly needs to be filled. I appeal to you, O my Lord, now to fill it.

I am weak in faith; I pray that you would strengthen me. I am cold in compassion for others. Make me hot and fervent, that my love may extend unto my neighbor.

I have no firm faith, and I do not always trust in you. O Lord help me! Increase my faith and confidence.

In you have I hidden the treasure of all good things. I am poor; you are rich. Therefore you came, that you might have mercy on the poor.

I am a sinner; you are righteous. Surely I have an abundance of sins, but in you is all fullness and grace. Amen.

— *Martin Luther*

RIP OUT THE WORST; REPLACE IT WITH THE BEST

O my Maker, rip out of me any rash boldness or contempt of others, any stubbornness and negligence, laziness, and dullness. Take from me any blindness of heart, obstinacy of mind, or contempt of the good.

Help me never to ignore wholesome advice, or offend with my tongue, or falsely accuse the innocent, or act violently against the powerless, or neglect the weak. May I never behave cruelly to my family, disrespect my friends, or turn away from my neighbor.

My merciful God, I beg you in your beloved Son, bless me with works of mercy and zeal of godliness to suffer with the afflicted, minister to the needy, and encourage the miserable. Enable me to counsel those who stray, and to comfort the sorrowful, relieve the oppressed, nourish the poor, and cherish those who mourn.

Help me to forgive those who owe me, pardon those who wrong me, and love those who hate me. May I always return good for evil, and despise no one—but instead honor all and imitate the good. Show me how to beware of evil, turn from vice and embrace virtue, remain patient in the face of adversity, and maintain humility in times of prosperity.

Help me to guard the door of my mouth, despise worldly things, and earnestly to thirst after the heavenly.

Amen.

— Book of Christian Prayers of 1578

LET YOUR SPIRIT POSSESS MY HEART

Gracious Father, let your Holy Spirit take possession of my heart, that I may trust in you only, love you above all things, keep your commandments, and cling to you forever. Amen.

— Myles Coverdale

You have chosen us as priests

Almighty God, since you have chosen us as your priests, we do not offer animal sacrifices, but we dedicate ourselves to you.

May we eagerly leave behind any uncleanness and purify ourselves from all that would defile us. Then we can rightly perform the sacred office of priest, and conduct ourselves towards you with decency and purity.

Give us strength also to abstain from every evil work, and from all fraud and cruelty towards other believers. As we deal with one another this way we will prove through our whole life that you are certainly our Father, that you are ruling us by your Spirit, and that true and holy fellowship exists between us.

Help us to live justly with one another, to show respect to each other, and so demonstrate that we are members of your only-begotten Son—owned by him when he appears for the redemption of his people, and gathering us into his heavenly kingdom. Amen.

— *John Calvin*

Keep us hurrying down the path

Almighty God, since you have made yourself known to us so plainly, not only by the Law and Prophets in your Scriptures, but also by your only-begotten Son, the knowledge of your truth ought to have already struck deep roots in us.

Grant that we may continue firm and constant in the work you have set aside for us—your holy vocation. Help us to make continued progress down that path, and always hurry onward to the goal.

Would you also humble us under your mighty hand, so we may know that we are disciplined under our parent? Help us to learn from your discipline until we are ultimately purified from all our failings and we come to enjoy that immortal life which has been made known to us by Christ.

Then we will be able fully to rejoice in you. Amen.

— John Calvin

LORD, WE WANT TO SERVE YOU

I pray in the name of our Lord Jesus Christ that you would fill our hearts with true faith. In this present world, joined to you in faith, grant that we may serve you as we ought. And after our departure out of this life, may we forever live with you in whom we believe.

To you be praise and glory forever, amen.

— Heinrich Bullinger

DRAW ME CLOSE IN YOUR LOVE

Sweet Lord, do not pass from me. Stay with me in your sweetness. For only your presence is comfort and relief to me, and only your absence leaves me sorrowful.

Holy Spirit, you inspire wherever you choose. Draw me to yourself, so I will totally reject in my heart all things of this world.

Light up my heart with your love so that it will burn forever on your altar. Come, I beg you, my sweet and true joy. Come, sweetness I so desire. Come, my beloved; you are all my comfort.

True love does not leave a loving soul to dwell in itself, alone, but draws it forth to its beloved.

Amen.

—*John Wycliffe*

LET US BELONG TO YOU COMPLETELY

O Lord our God, we humbly ask that you would grant us the grace of your Holy Spirit. May the Spirit's bright beams shine into our hearts to expel every mist of blindness, darkness, and ignorance. Please enable us to see the mysteries of your will and the wondrous things of your law!

Lord, we humbly ask that you would humble us in ourselves. Then as we see and know our own unworthiness and unrighteousness, we may be free of ourselves, unto you, and in you we may find rest for our souls.

Increase, O Lord, our knowledge in you and our obedience to you. Fill this our knowledge with the fruits of righteousness, so that in our faith, working by love, we may be known truly to belong to you.

Amen.

— *Henry Airay*

MAY WE FINISH THE RACE STRONG

O Lord Jesus Christ, you go before us and protect us. Now grant us grace to continue faithfully in the work you have set aside for us.

Help us to continue in your service, and never in our laziness regard it as tedious. Help us also never to back away from the passionate pursuit of your holy calling.

Instead, help us to we stand strong as we watch and pray, and with a constant mind stand up to any physical challenges. Help us to show patience in adversity and not fear anyone's verbal attacks.

At the same time, may we never desire this world's praise and honor. Help us only to seek your eternal rewards, and never turn from the way of the cross as a result of wealth—or trouble. Under the banner of Jesus, and with true patience, meekness, and obedience, may we finish our life strong, with your blessing. Amen.

— *Myles Coverdale*

I COMMIT TO YOU MY LIFE AND FUTURE

Lord, you are the hope of everyone on the earth, the hope of those on the broad seas. Our ancestors hoped in you, and you delivered them. They waited on you, and were not disappointed. You have been my hope since I was small, since I was an infant, since I was born.

Be my hope now and evermore, and my portion in the land of the living. My hope is in your name, in your word, and in your work. Do not disappoint me!

Remember your whole creation for good. Visit the world in your compassion. Remember us all, you who preserve and love us. Have pity on us. You who died and rose again to be Lord of the dead and living, we live and die to you. You are our Lord.

Helper of the helpless, a refuge in time of trouble, remember all those who need your help. God of grace and truth, establish all who stand in truth and grace, restore all who are sick in heresy and sin. Remember your congregation, which you have bought and redeemed.

Grant to all believers one heart and one soul. Set in order the things that fall short. Strengthen what remains, which you were ready to cast away, which was ready to die.

Lord of the harvest, send forth laborers. Help our pastors to rightly divide the word of truth, and to walk rightly in it. Grant to your Christian people strength to obey and submit themselves to you, King of nations, to the ends of the earth.

Strengthen those countries that follow your ways, and
scatter the nations that delight in war. Make wars to cease
in all the earth! Grant holy wisdom to judges and rulers.
Bless our children that they may increase in wisdom as
in stature, and in favor with you and others. Help me to
speak peace to my relations, and to seek their good.

Lord, Scripture tells us that those who neglect their own are
worse than an unbeliever. Remember all those in my household.
Peace be to my house, and the Son of peace be upon all in it.

You who grant the prayers of your servants, be merciful
to all who remember me in their prayers, or whom I have
promised to remember in mine. Have mercy on them, O
Lord, and also on me.

Remember the hungry and thirsty, the sick and those
who lack clothes, prisoners, foreigners, the homeless, all
in extreme age and weakness, those who are troubled by
unclean spirits or tempted to suicide, those who despair
or are sick in soul or body, the fainthearted, all in prison
and chains, all under sentence of death, orphans, widows,
travelers, pregnant women, servants, mineworkers, and those
who are lonely. ... How excellent is your mercy, O God!

We place our trust under the shadow of your wings. May
you bless and keep us, show us your light, and be merciful
to us. Give us your peace. O Lord, I commit to you my
body, soul, and mind, my thoughts, prayers, and vows, my
senses, words, and my works. I commit my life and my
death, my family and friends, my neighbors, my country,
and all who follow you. Amen.

— *Lancelot Andrewes*

GRANT ME A PLACE UNDER YOUR FEET

Hosanna in the highest!

Remember me with favor, Lord. Visit me with your salvation, so I experience the happiness of your chosen, and rejoice in the gladness of your people. Let me give thanks along with the people of your inheritance.

There is glory which will be revealed. When the judge comes, some of us will behold your face with joy. They will be placed on the right and hear those most welcome words: "Come you who are blessed."

They will be caught up in clouds to meet the Lord. They will enter into joy. They will enjoy the sight of him, and they will be with him forever. These alone, only these, are blessed among the people.

Grant me the most humble place under their feet— under the feet of your elect, of the lowest among them. And for this to happen, let me find grace in your sight to have grace, to serve you acceptably with reverence and godly fear.

Let me find that second grace, and not receive the first grace in vain. Do not let me fall short or neglect it, so as to fall from it. But stir up that grace so I may increase in it and abide in it until the end of my life.

Make perfect for me what is lacking of your gifts. Of faith, help my unbelief. Of hope, settle it in my life, despite my trembling. Of love, kindle its smoking ember. Increase your love in my heart, so I may love my friend in you, and my enemy for you.

You who give grace to the humble-minded, give me also grace to be humble-minded. You who never fail those who fear you, knit my heart to you, that I may fear your name. You who are my fear and hope, let me fear nothing more than you.

As I would that others should do to me, even so may I do to them—not to think of myself more highly than I ought to think, but to think clearly.

Shine on those who sit in darkness, and in the shadow of death. Guide our feet into the way of peace, that we may be like-minded with one another. Help us to think and walk rightly, that we may lift each other up, and glorify you with one voice.

Amen.

— *Lancelot Andrewes*

Help me to get my priorities straight

Lord, would you first pardon me for cherishing my affections. I have obeyed these superfluous desires and they have taken deep root. They are too lively in me.

Pull them up by the roots out of my heart. Train me to weaken the main roots of those desires, so the by-roots and branches may then lose all their power.

May your grace daily put to death my intense desire for pleasant things: wealth, glory, liberty, popularity, food and drink, clothes, leisure—and yes, even life itself. Weaken my distaste of more grievous things so that I become more patient in adversity.

Make me forever obedient and ready to your good will in all things. Help me to serve you willingly and from the heart, doing whatever pleases you. Because even as we grow from self-gratification to self-denial, we will always find enough challenges when more bitter and weighty crosses come.

Your Son, our Savior—who was always accustomed to doing your will—prayed earnestly and often, "Not my will, but yours be done." He declared his humanity in those words. And if Jesus himself said that, we surely will have our hands full with great temptations as we wholly resign ourselves to you—given our own cradle-to-grave corrupt natures.

So grant that your grace and Holy Spirit will work as they should in me. May I daily grow accustomed to denying myself in the easy and pleasant things of life. Then I can come to Christ with a surrendered will, anticipating your mercy, and obeying you always with readiness and willingness. Then I can do whatever most pleases you, through Jesus Christ our Lord, amen.

— John Bradford

I WANT NO OTHER GOD THAN YOU

Lord, in your goodness and mercy forgive my idolatry. And as you deliver me from bowing to sticks and stones, so, dear Father, deliver me from all other bowing—bowing to my own will and affections.

I desire no other God in my heart but you. I desire to serve no other God but you, just as your word commands.

I should look for all good things only at your hands. I should put all my trust in you, be thankful to you, love you, fear you, obey you, and call upon your holy name in all my needs. And so should I give this faith, love, fear, obedience, thankfulness, and prayer to none other (no, not in my heart), but only to you.

So open my eyes to see your will. Give me a will to love your way with all my heart, and a heart to obey you faithfully, for your dear Son's sake, Jesus Christ our Lord. Amen.

— John Bradford

How can we find our way home?

Our Father in heaven, we, your children upon earth, are separated from you in exile. What a great gulf is between you and us! How may we ever get home to you in our homeland?

O Father, it is sadly true. We recognize our guilt, but be a gracious father and do not enter into judgment with us. Instead, grant us grace that we may live so that your holy name may be purified in us. Let us think, speak, do, possess, or undertake nothing unless it results in your honor and praise—that before all things your honor and name, not our own vain honor and name, may be found in us. Grant that we may love, fear, and honor you as children do a father.

Father, it is true. We feel ourselves inclined to sin. The world, flesh, and the devil seeks to reign in us, and would banish your honor and name. Deliver us from our exile! Let your kingdom come, that sin may be cast out and we may become righteous and acceptable to you. May you alone rule in us. And as we submit to you all our strength of soul and body, may we become your kingdom.

We are sorry that we cannot bear your healing hand or understand its purpose. Father, grant us grace, and help us to consent to your divine will. Even if it is painful to us, continue to chastise, pierce, strike, and burn. Do whatever you will, only that your will and not ours may be done.

Restrain, dear Father, and allow us to undertake or accomplish nothing under the guidance of our own opinion, desire, or purpose. For our will is opposed to yours. Your will alone is good, although it does not appear so, while ours is evil, although it may seem good.

Father, it is surely true: "Not by might shall a man prevail" (1 Sam 2:9). And who can remain before your hand unless you yourself strengthen and comfort? So lay hold of us, dear Father. Work your will, that we may become your kingdom, to your praise and honor.

But as you deal with us this way, strengthen us with your holy word. Give us our daily bread. Give to our hearts your dear Son Jesus Christ, the true bread from heaven. Strengthened by him, we may joyfully stand and agree that your will be done, while our will is defeated and put to death.

Give grace also to the whole kingdom of Christ. Send us well-taught pastors and preachers who will not seek to comfort us by sowing worthless fancies, but who will teach us your holy gospel and Jesus Christ.

Father, have mercy and do not deny us the precious bread—though it grieves us that we do not do as you have commanded. Be patient with us poor children, dismiss our guilt, and do not enter into judgment with us, for in your sight no one is justified. Recall your promise to forgive those who have forgiven their debtors. Not that by such forgiveness we become worthy of your forgiveness, but you are true and have graciously promised forgiveness to all who forgive their neighbors. We trust in your promise.

We are weak and sick, and the many temptations of the flesh and the world are great. Hold us, dear Father. Do not let us fall into temptation and sin again, but grant us grace, so we may remain steadfast and fight bravely until our end. Without your grace and help we can do nothing.

Deliver us from evil, dear Father, so that we may be your kingdom, to praise, honor, and bless you for all eternity. And since you have taught and commanded us to pray this way, and promised to hear us, we trust and are assured that you will grant this prayer—to the honor of your truth, with grace and mercy.

To God alone be honor and glory, amen.

— *Martin Luther*

A soldier's prayer of dedication

Heavenly Father, here I am, according to your divine will, in the work and service of my commanding officer, which I owe first to you and then to my commander for your sake.

I thank your grace and mercy that you have placed me into a position which I am sure is not sin, but right and pleasing obedience to your will. But because I know and have learned from your gracious word that none of our good works can help us and no one is saved as a soldier but only as a Christian, I will rely not at all on this obedience and work of mine.

Instead, I put myself freely at the service of your will. And I believe from the heart that only the innocent blood of your dear Son, my Lord Jesus Christ, redeems and saves me. He has shed his blood for me in obedience to your holy will.

On this truth I stand. On this truth I live and die. On this truth I fight and do all.

Dear Lord God and Father, preserve and strengthen this faith in me, by your Spirit. Amen.

— Martin Luther

I embrace only you, sweet Jesus

Lord, you are love. Be also tears to me, by day and by night. For unless we are punished first by weeping, we cannot come to the sweetness of your love.

Everlasting love, inflame my mind to love you, my God. May my mind only burn to your callings.

O good Jesus! You must now be felt and not seen. Enter into the inmost recesses of my soul. Come into my heart and fill it entirely with your most clear sweetness.

Make my mind drink deeply of the fervent wine of your sweet love. Then I will forget all evils, vain visions, and scornful imaginations. Then I will embrace only you as I rejoice in my Lord Jesus.

Amen.

— John Wycliffe

I wholly commit myself to you

Dear eternal, heavenly Father, I call on you from the depths of my heart. Do not let me turn from you, but keep me in you truth all the way to my end.

Keep my heart and mouth. Guard me, so I may never separate from you, even on account of approaching sorrow, suffering, or anguish. Help me to remain cheerful and glad in my distress.

Eternal God and dear Father, teach me as your poor, unworthy child to keep to your ways and paths. This is my sincere desire, that through your power I may press even unto death, through all sorrows, sufferings, anguish. and pain. In this let me persevere, O God, that I may not be separated from your love.

There are many who now walk in this way, but the cup of suffering is given them to drink. We are also accused of false doctrine, in order to draw us from Christ our Lord. But I lift up my soul to you, O God, and I trust in you in every disaster.

Do not let me be put to shame, so my enemy would exalt himself over me in this earth. I wait for you with great desire, O dear heavenly Father. Prepare us like the five wise virgins (Matthew 25:2), as we wait for the bridegroom with his heavenly hosts.

Heavenly King, feed and refresh us according to the Spirit with your heavenly food, which never perishes but remains in life eternal. If you should hold back your food from us, all that we do would be in vain and would perish.

But through your grace we trust in you. We trust that we will not fail. I do not doubt in the least your power. I honor your judgment. You will abandon no one who holds firmly to you in faith, and seeks to walk in your true ways.

I rejoice with the believers in the Lord Jesus Christ! Increase our love and faith, and comfort us by your holy word, in which we may firmly trust. I commit myself to you and to your church. Be my protector today, for your holy name's sake. O my Father, let it be done through Jesus Christ, amen.

— *Anna of Freiburg*

Just passing through?

Almighty God, our life is only for a moment. No, actually, it is only vanity and smoke! So teach us to cast all our cares upon you, and to depend on you.

Teach us to be ready to put aside our lives, especially for the testimony of your glory. May we be prepared to depart as soon as you call us from this world.

And may the hope of eternal life be so fixed in our hearts that we willingly leave this world—looking forward with all our mind toward that blessed eternity which you have told us is laid up for us in heaven, through the gospel, obtained for us through the blood of your only-begotten Son, amen.

— *John Calvin*

Grant me a mind to know you

Merciful God, help me to desire fervently those things that please you. Help me to search them wisely, to know them truly, and to fulfill them perfectly, to the praise and glory of your name.

Order my living so that I may do what you require of me. And give me grace to gain what is best for my soul.

Lord, make my way sure and straight to you. May I give you thanks in prosperity, and be patient in adversity. May I only rejoice in the things that draw me closer to you, and be sorry for those things that draw me away from you.

May I desire to please no one, and fear to displease no one, except you, Lord.

Let all worldly things be repulsive to me, for you. Do not let me be happy with any joy that is without you, and do not let me desire anything besides you.

May labor that is done for you delight me, and let all rest weary me which is not in you. Help me to lift up my heart to you often. And when I fall, make me think on you.

My God, make me humble without pretending, happy without insincerity, sad without mistrust, earnest without dullness, true without deceitfulness. Help me to fear you without desperation, trust you without presumption, teach through word and example without mocking, and obey without arguing. Help me to be patient without grudging and pure without corruption.

My loving Lord and God, give me a waking heart, so no curious thought would withdraw me from you. Let my heart be so strong, that no unworthy affection will draw me backward, and so stable, that no tribulation will break it.

Grant me a mind to know you, Lord. Give me diligence to seek you. Conversation to please you. And hope to embrace you.

I pray all this for the sake of that immaculate lamb, our only Savior Jesus Christ—to whom be all honor and glory with the Father and the Holy Spirit, three persons and one God. Amen.

— Primer of 1559

Keep us on the right path

Almighty God, morning and evening you continue to invite us to yourself. You never tire of encouraging us to repent. You testify that you are ready to reconcile with us, provided we flee to your mercy.

O grant that we may not close our ears and reject your great kindness. Rather, by keeping in mind your free election—the biggest favor you have ever shown us—we may then devote ourselves to you. Your name will then be glorified throughout our entire life.

And if we ever at any time turn aside from you, may we quickly return to the right path. May we quickly submit again to your holy guidance. May we give evidence once more that you have chosen and called us, and that we will continue in the hope of that salvation to which you have invited us, and which is prepared for us in heaven, through Christ our Lord. Amen.

— John Calvin

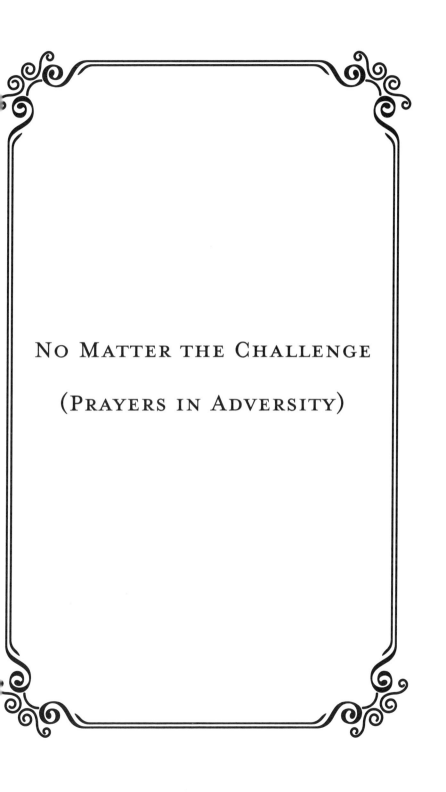

No Matter the Challenge

(Prayers in Adversity)

Help in this trouble

Help, Lord God. Help in this trouble! I think death is at the door. Stand before me, Christ, for you have overcome death!

I cry to you: If it is your will, remove the dart that wounds me—a wound that allows me not even an hour's rest.

But if it is your will for death to take me in the midst of my days … so let it be. I lack nothing. I am your vessel to make or break.

And if you take my spirit from this earth, do it so that I will not grow worse, or burden the good lives of others. Amen.

— Huldrych Zwingli

You sent not a Jonah, but Jesus

Almighty God, you did not send us a Jonah when we were alienated from every hope of salvation. You gave your Son to be our teacher, to show to us the clear way of salvation.

You called us to repentance not by threats and terrors, but you allured us with kindness to the hope of eternal life, with a pledge of your fatherly love.

May we never reject such an amazing favor, Lord, but may we obey you willingly and from the heart.

The condition you set before us in your gospel may
seem hard, and bearing the cross seems bitter to
our flesh. Still may we always obey you and present
ourselves to you as a sacrifice.

Then, once all the hindrances of this world are overcome,
may we move ahead in the course of our holy calling, until
we are ultimately gathered into your heavenly kingdom
under the guidance of Christ your Son, our Lord. Amen.

— John Calvin

As illness descends

Comfort me, Lord God, and reassure me as illness
descends. The illness increases, as pain and fear seize soul
and body. Come with your grace, for it is our only relief
for those who set their hopes and heart desires on you,
despising all gain and loss.

Now I cannot say another word. My senses are broken.
It is time for you to take over this fight. I am not strong
enough to resist the devil's schemes or false hand.

Still, no matter how he rages, my spirit will ever abide
with you.

Amen.

— Huldrych Zwingli

Be glorified in my life or death

O Lord, if this is the hour you have set for me, your will be done. Only please do not rebuke me in your anger!

Lord, my dearest God, you know how willingly I would have shed my blood for your word, but perhaps I am not worthy. Your will be done. If it be your will that I die, may your name be glorified by life or death. If it had been possible I would have wished to live longer for the sake of the believers, Lord, for the sake of your elect, but if the hour is come, you are the Lord of life and death.

My dearest God, you have led me into this business. You know my life is all about your truth and your word. Do not let our enemies be glorified, but glorify your holy name against the enemies of your most holy word.

Lord Jesus, you have given me the knowledge of your name. You know I believe that you are true God and our true mediator and savior. Be present with your Spirit in this hour.

Up to now, Lord, you have wonderfully kept me. Keep me still, if it is your will. My dearest God, you are always a God of sinners and those who are miserable. Help me!

Lord Jesus, you said to ask and you will receive, seek and you will find, knock and it will be opened unto you. Open now to the one who knocks!

Dearest God and Father, you have given me many thousand precious gifts above what you have given others.

I would have liked still to be used for the honor of your name and the good of your people. But your will be done, that you may be glorified by life or death. Amen.

— Martin Luther

RAISE US UP LIKE A GRAPEVINE

Lord, you diligently train us up, like a dear and precious grapevine whose care is passed on from generation to generation.

Grant that we would not produce wild grapes, and that our fruit may not be bitter and unpleasant to you. Help us to build our whole life in obedience to your law, that all our thoughts and actions may be pleasant and sweet fruits for you.

And as there is always some sin mixed up with our works—even when we desire to serve you sincerely and from the heart—grant that all the stains in what we do may be cleansed and washed away by the sacrifice of your Son.

In the end, may we be a sweet-smelling sacrifice to you, through Christ Jesus, who has reconciled us to you and obtained pardon even for our works. Amen.

—John Calvin

A DYING PRAYER

O heavenly Father, my gracious God and Father of our
Lord Jesus Christ, you are the God of all consolation.
And I give you my heartfelt thanks that you have revealed
to me your Son Jesus Christ, whom I believe, whom I
profess, whom I love, and whom I glorify.

I appeal to you, Lord Jesus Christ, to receive my soul. O
my gracious Heavenly Father, though I be taken out of this
life, though I must lay down this frail body, yet I certainly
know that I will live with you eternally, and that I cannot
be taken out of your hand.

Into your hand I commit my spirit. You have redeemed
me, O Lord, God of truth. Amen.

— *Martin Luther*

HELP ME TO DO AS YOU COMMAND

Dear Lord, David said that your eyes are on the righteous,
and your ears are open to their cries—but your face is
against those who do evil.

I am your friend if I do what you command.

It is true, dear Lord, that Christ was given to us, and died
for us—but not so we could live according to our wicked
lusts and sinful will, but according to your good will.
According to your word. And according to your command.

Lord, I know that you are no less righteous than good.
I know that you hate evil, and love good. I know you
are kind to the good, but that in due time you will be a
righteous judge to the wicked.

What did the pure blood of the eternal covenant demand
of Cain and Judah, because they despised your grace and
excluded themselves from the merits of your Son? And
what good was it for Pilate, Herod, or Caiaphas to have
seen your fountain of grace, Jesus Christ—no actually,
touched him—and yet they condemned the Lamb, the King
of glory, to a cursed death of the cross!

But they who keep your covenant and preserve your
testimony like Noah, Abraham, Isaac, and Jacob did, to
them your ways are peace and joy, mercy, kindness, and
truth, amen.

— *Menno Simons*

Your will is mine

O my God and Lord, I am altogether lacking in that which
I owe you, and it is not within my own power to secure
it. Therefore I pray that you would graciously work in
me the fulfillment of what you command—and command
whatever you will. Amen.

— *Martin Luther*

WE WILL ONE DAY SING WITH SIMEON

Almighty God, bend our hearts into true, constant, and healthy repentance, that we may be the children of God. I pray that when it is time for us to depart from this life, we may all, in agreement with Simeon and from the bottom of our hearts, joyfully sing:

"Lord, now you are letting your servant depart in peace, according to your word; for my eyes have seen your salvation that you have prepared in the presence of all peoples, a light for revelation for the Gentiles, and for glory to your people Israel" (Luke 2:29–32).

Amen.

— Niels Hemmingsen

ON EARTH AS IT IS IN HEAVEN

Lord, since you are Father and King over all, and we are your children, make us obedient to seek and to do your will, as the angels do in heaven. May none of us seek our own will, but all yours. But if rulers command what is contrary to your will, then help us to stand fast by your word, and to offer ourselves to suffer rather than to obey.

You know everything, Lord. Your son Jesus gave us an example when he desired (if it had been possible) that that cup of bitter death might have departed from him, saying, "Yet not as I will, but as you will."

So if we pray to you in our temptations and adversities,
and you see a better way to your glory and our profit, then
your will be done—not ours.

Amen.

— *William Tyndale*

SO GREAT A KINDNESS

Almighty God, up to now you have shown us so many
favors, ever since the time you were pleased to adopt us as
your people.

Now grant that we may not forget so great a kindness,
nor be led away by the enticements of Satan, nor seek for
ourselves novelties that will ultimately wreck us.

Instead, may we continue fixed in our obedience to you.
May we daily call on you, and drink of the fullness of
your bounty.

At the same time may we strive to serve you from the
heart, and glorify your name, and so prove that we are
wholly devoted to you. Amen.

— *John Calvin*

EVEN WHEN WE ARE ALMOST BURIED

Almighty God, you once demonstrated your infinite power through your servant Jonah. Even when he was almost sunk down to hell, you raised him to yourself—to the place where he did not stop praying and calling on you.

Now grant that we may also raise our hearts and minds to you, even in the trials we face daily. May we never cease to recognize how close you are to us.

Help us to keep struggling and to never surrender the hope of your mercy—even when the signs of your wrath appear, or when our sins thrust themselves before our eyes and drive us to despair.

Then, when the contest is finished, we can freely and fully give thanks to you, and praise your infinite goodness that we daily experience through trials. And then we may at last come into that blessed rest which is laid up for us in heaven, through Christ our Lord. Amen.

— John Calvin

HELP US TO CONTINUE IN OBEDIENCE

Since you have stooped down to adopt us as your people, and to unite us in your only Son, help us to continue pure and untainted in our obedience to your gospel. Help us never to turn aside to those corruptions which pull apart that sacred bond, confirmed between us by the blood of your Son.

Help us to persevere in serving you, so that our whole life and all our actions may be evidence of that holy calling, laid up for us as the hope of eternal salvation, until we at last come to own that kingdom which has been obtained for us by so great a price. There we will enjoy the fruit of our faith, sincerity, and perseverance through Christ our Lord, amen.

— John Calvin

A PRAYER FOR PATIENCE

When you lived in this world, Lord Jesus, you showed perfect patience. You suffered quietly through not only the spiteful words, but also the cruel deeds of your enemies. You forgave and prayed for those who treated you the worst.

Meek and loving Lamb of God, give me grace to follow the example of your patience. Help me to quietly bear the worst words against me, and endure when I am mistreated. And then help me to forgive and pray for anyone who mistreats me—even to do them good. And may I never take my own revenge. Vengeance belongs to you.

Lord, you bring to right those who suffer wrong. So as I patiently endure all evils, may I afterward reign with you in glory. Amen.

— Thomas Becon

Lead us to your kingdom, Lord

Lord God, I will praise you now and until my end. You have given me faith, by which I have learned to know you. You send me your divine word, which I am able to find and understand that it is from pure grace. From you, O God, I firmly hope that it will not return to you empty (Isaiah 55:11).

O Lord, strengthen my heart; it rejoices because I know your will. When I have felt the heavy load of sin in me, which severely troubled me, I would have perished and suffered everlasting pain if you had not come to me with the word of your divine grace.

For this I will now magnify and praise your glorious name forever. You always prove yourself to be a merciful, dear Father.

Do not cast me off, but receive me as your child. I cry unto you for help, O Father, that I may be your child and heir. Strengthen my faith. Otherwise, if your help did not lift me up, my building would soon fall.

Do not forget me, O Lord, but be with me always. May your Holy Spirit protect and teach me, that in all my sufferings I would always receive your comfort. And so valiantly fighting in this conflict, I may gain the victory.

The enemy fights against me and would drive me from the battlefield if he could. But you, O Lord, give me the victory. He came against me with sharp weapons, with false doctrine and restrictions. But you had compassion on me, and helped your child with your grace and powerful hand. You helped me overcome. You heard me, and

quickly came to help. You turned back my enemies. So I
will sing praises to your name in my heart, and forever
spread abroad the grace which has come to me.

Now I pray to you, Father, for all your children. Preserve
us forever from all the enemies of our souls. I must not
trust in the flesh, which perishes—but I will firmly trust in
your word. This is my hope and strength, on which I rely.

Lead us into your everlasting kingdom, as I firmly trust
that you will, and finish your holy work in us. Grant us
strength to the end. Amen.

— Georg Blaurock

ALL THE HELP WE CAN GET

Almighty God, you have spared nothing to help us onward
in the course of our faith. But despite that, with our
laziness we hardly advance a step.

So help us now strive to benefit more from all the helps
you have provided us. Awaken us more fully with the Law,
the Prophets, the voice of John the Baptist, and especially
the doctrine of your only-begotten Son.

And may we not only hurry to Jesus, but may we also
move ahead constantly on our course, persevering until
we ultimately receive the victory and the crown of our
calling—because you have promised an eternal inheritance
in heaven to all who do not give up, but who wait for the
coming of the great Redeemer. Amen.

— John Calvin

LET ADVERSITIES ENERGIZE MY FAITH

O blessed Jesus, let me pass through fiery trials here, and let me even be bitterly persecuted in this world, as long as you just spare me in the world that is to come.

Blessed Jesus, you often spare us by apparently casting us away from yourself. Grant that by your merciful stripes upon us we may be brought back again to you. Afflict and chastise the outward person, if only the inward person may in that way grow in strength and power.

Merciful Jesus, be with me to help me in all my conflicts with myself. Direct me in my struggles, and crown me with glorious victory. Whatever adversities I may suffer in this life, let them serve to energize and increase my faith. Strengthen my feeble faith, O blessed Jesus, for you promised to do so by your prophet: "As one whom his mother comforts, so I will comfort you" (Isaiah 66:13).

As a mother cherishes and nourishes with more tender and anxious care her newborn infant because of its very helplessness, so, merciful Jesus, encourage and strengthen my soul because of the very weakness and feebleness of my faith. Grant that the inward consolation of your grace may have more influence and power upon me than all the contradictions of ungodly persons and of the devil himself.

Lord Jesus, you are the Good Samaritan. Pour into the gaping wounds of my sins the stinging wine of your just judgments. But at the same time, add the soothing oil of your divine encouragement. Increase the burden of the cross I already bear, if you will, but grant me also the strength to bear it. Amen.

— *Johann Gerhard*

Keep me on your path

O Lord, your divine grace has shone around me, your word has taught me, and your Holy Spirit has drawn me to abandon the ungodly road.

The world once loved me and had captured my affections. I was ungodly and I carried the banner of unrighteousness for many years. I was a leader in all kinds of foolishness. But when I saw that it was all just pompous pride, I renounced the ungodliness of this world to seek you and your kingdom … which will abide in eternity.

O Lord, comfort me. Preserve your troubled servant, for I am poor and wretched. My sins rise up against me, the whole world hates and mocks me. I am persecuted, cursed, and slandered. Even my dearest friends forsake me, and those who were near to me now stand far off.

Have mercy on me, Lord. Only you can preserve me. Lead me in the right way so I do not stumble in the dark mountains. Deceit and hypocrisy are everywhere.

Teach me your truth and do not cast me away from your presence, Lord. I am in the midst of lions and bears that seek to destroy my soul and would pull me from the way of truth. Strengthen me and keep me in your way, Lord, for I know that it is the infallible truth and the sure way of peace. Amen.

— *Menno Simons*

YOU TURN ADVERSITY FOR MY GOOD

Lord God, a sparrow cannot fall to the ground except by your will and permission. So…

It is by your will and permission that I should be in this misery and adversity.

You discipline me with adversity—not to destroy me and cast me away, but to call me to repentance and save me. "For the Lord disciplines the one he loves" (Hebrews 12:6).

Affliction and adversity bring about patience, and whoever patiently bears tribulation is made to be like our Savior Christ, our head.

And in all tribulation or adversity I am assured of comfort from your gracious hand. For you have commanded me to call on you in the time of tribulation, and you have promised to hear and comfort me.

Grant me therefore in all trouble and adversity to be quiet—not impatient or murmuring, and not discouraged or desperate. Help me to praise and magnify you, and to put my whole trust and confidence in you. For you never abandon those who trust in you, but you work everything for the best to those who love you and who seek the glory of your holy name.

To you be glory forever and ever. Amen.

— *Primer of 1559*

We wait for you, Redeemer

Almighty God, today we are not looking for a redeemer
to deliver us from our day-to-day miseries. The redeemer
we seek only carries on warfare under the banner of the
cross—until he appears to us from heaven to gather us into
his blessed kingdom.

Help us to patiently bear today's evils and troubles. And as
Christ once for all poured forth the blood of the new and
eternal covenant, and gave us in communion a symbol of
that covenant, may we have confidence in such a sacred
seal and never doubt that he will always comfort and
provide us with the clear fruit of his reconciliation.

After supporting us for a season through the burdens that
now weigh us down, he will gather us to a blessed and
perfect glory—bought for us with his own blood and daily
set before us in the gospel, and laid up for us in heaven,
where we will one day come to enjoy that glory. Amen.

— John Calvin

An appeal for healing

Lord God, heavenly Father, who has commanded us
to pray for the sick, we appeal to you through Jesus
Christ, your only beloved Son: deliver this your servant
from sickness and from the hand of the devil. Spare, O
Lord, her soul, which, together with her body, you have
purchased and redeemed from the power of sin, death,
and the devil. Amen.

— Martin Luther

WE DESERVE THE WORST, BUT THANK YOU FOR THE BEST

Our head and the one who goes before us, we are so unlike you! We are so far from right and true humility, when we are offended by fellow believers at the slightest wrong or unadvised word. And where we should give thanks for being rebuked for our own good, we are impatient and aggrieved!

O Lord Jesus Christ, help us to consider your holy sacrifice, so that it might produce fruit in us. Make us patient in the face of hurt and disapproval. Teach us by your example not to fear the rants and persecution of wicked people. Help us not to be discouraged by any wrongful accusations.

Teach us to see our own depravity, and how justly we are reviled and despised for our sins. Have mercy, O Lord, on our imperfection. You were reviled that you might take from us everlasting shame. You were beaten to deliver us from the beating we deserved for our sins. You were spit upon and mocked to bring us from everlasting confusion to everlasting honor.

So strengthen our minds, Lord, that in lowly shame we may patiently suffer and bear the hard words and checks that others give us for our sins and offenses. After all, you endured many more and much more false accusations and rebukes for us vile sinners. And you bore it all with the highest patience.

May the hard blows you endured ease our pains. May that scornful blindfolding of your eyes restrain us from hardheartedness and conceit. Let the vile spitting on your holy face expel all carnal lusts from us. And may it teach us not to regard the outward appearance, but to hold and keep in honor the virtues of the soul.

May all the undeserved scorn and ridicule you experienced drive from us all our corrupt or degraded ways. May that rejection of your worthiness drive all desire from us of honor in this world. May it move us instead to pursue things which, in this world, are looked down upon.

Give us, Lord, strong victory in all patience. From our heart-roots may we acknowledge and confess ourselves to be most worthy of all contempt and slander, of all rebuke, shame, and punishment. Amen.

— Myles Coverdale

SAVE US FROM ANGER AND REVENGE

Our Lord Jesus Christ, you told us that whoever is angry with his brother is guilty and deserving of judgment.

In your great mercy, help us never to undo ourselves through anger or a desire for revenge. Help us always to remember not only your godly commandment—which charges us to do well to those who hate us, and to pray for those who speak evil of us—but also that we keep in mind your holy example. You prayed for those who cruelly crucified you.

To you, with the Father and the Holy Spirit, be glory everlasting. Amen.

— Primer of 1559

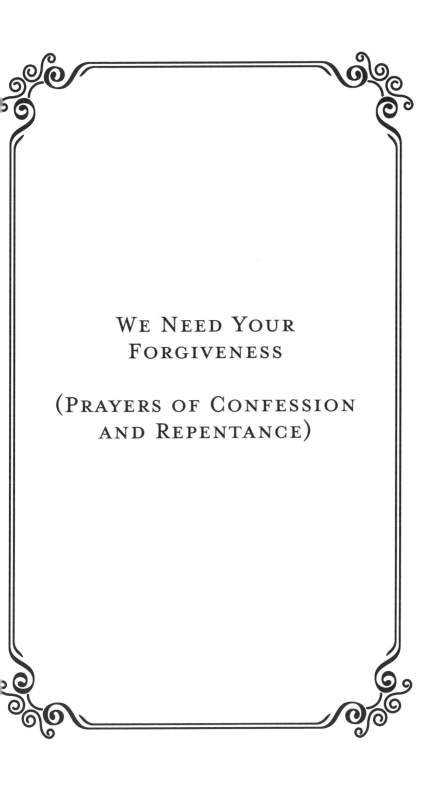

We Need Your Forgiveness

(Prayers of Confession and Repentance)

REMOVE THE FLOOD OF WICKED THOUGHTS

Lord, as we add day to day, so we add sin to sin. If a righteous person sins seven times a day, I sin seventy times seven! What a wonderful, horrible thing, Lord.

I conceal nothing. I make no excuses.

But I turn with groans from my evil ways, and I return into my heart, and with all my heart I turn to you. You are the God of those who repent and the Savior of sinners. And evening by evening I will return from the innermost marrow of my soul, and out of the deep of my soul I will cry to you:

I have sinned, O Lord, against you, heavily against you. I have destroyed myself!

I repent, Lord. I repent! Spare me. I repent; help my lack of repentance. Give me hope and comfort me.

Remember what I am made of: the work of your hands, your likeness, your blood price, a name from your Name, a sheep of your pasture, a child of the covenant. Did you make your own image and likeness for nothing? Yes for nothing, if you destroy me.

So spare me, O Lord. Have mercy on me. Heal my soul, for I have sinned against you. Have mercy upon me in your great goodness. Do away with my offenses in the cloud of your mercy. Drain away the guilt, heal the wound, blot out the stains, deliver me from the shame, rescue me from the control of sin.

Lord, bring me out of my trouble and cleanse me from my secret faults. Protect me, your servant, from my most arrogant sins. Do not condemn me for wanderings of mind and idle words.

Remove the dark and muddy flood of foul and wicked thoughts, Lord. Whatever I have done wrong, pardon me in your mercy. Do not deal with me as my sins deserve. Look on me with mercy, and for the glory of your all-holy name, turn from me all those evils and miseries which my sins (and I) most certainly deserve.

Lord, tell me that my sins are forgiven, for your name's sake. No other name is given, by which we may be saved. Say to me, "My grace is sufficient." Tell my soul that you are my salvation.

Amen.

— *Lancelot Andrewes*

PLUCK US OUT OF THE PIT

Even if we have fallen to the bottom, Lord, reach down your arm after us. It is long and strong enough to pluck us out again.

Deliver us out of the flesh, the world, and the power of the devil. Deliver us from evil! And place us in your kingdom, to the place where we are beyond all jeopardy.

For yours is the kingdom and the power forever, amen.

— *William Tyndale*

How have I taken your name in vain?

Lord, the tongue is so hard to tame, yet we neglect it.
What might happen if we use it in your service? Though
others would never fault us, you hold us to a higher
standard if we take your name in vain.

You pour out your great mercies to me, and you offer them
still, but I am a terrible offender of this good commandment.

I have abused your name.

When I pray, I am not attentive, nor do I desire much the
thing for which I pray. After prayer I have not earnestly
looked for the good things I asked for. So when I receive
the answer, I am unthankful.

I read your word little and negligently, soon forgetting
what I do read.

I do not reprimand others when I hear them abuse your holy
word. I fear losing friends, or reputation, or even my life if
I were to confess your truth and your gospel—the name I
called upon when I was baptized. Sadly, I can hardly call to
light how many times I have now broken this your law.

This is a sin above other sins, that under your name, your
word, and your gospel, I play the hypocrite. I care more
about my own name than yours. For if someone spoke evil
of my name, it would grieve me, and I would defend it.

But I hear evil spoken of your name every day. I see your
name profaned by false doctrine and evil living—but it does

not grieve me. I do not try to fix these things in myself and in others. And why not? Good Lord, I love myself better than I love you, and I do not love you with my whole heart. Your first commandment does not have the place in my heart that it should have. It does not possess my heart, mind, and will as you require. For this reason alone I should be condemned.

Gracious God, what can I do? By taking your name in vain, I horribly offend you in so many ways. In praying and not praying. Reading and not reading. Speaking and not speaking. And in not confessing simply and from my heart your truth and your name—but regarding my own name far above yours.

Should I flee from you? That would add sin to sin. You want me to call on your holy name. You, who have given your dear Son as a mediator for us, so that through him we might find not only grace for the pardon of past sins, but also to obtain your Holy Spirit. You want us to understand and obey this holy precept forever.

So for his sake, dear God, please pardon those past and present sins of which this law accuses me. Most gracious Father, fill me and saturate me with your Holy Spirit to know and love your holy name, word, and truth in Jesus Christ. Grant that I may be zealous, wise, and constant. Sanctify my tongue from now on. Guide me with grace and your Spirit to publish, confess, and teach others your truth and gospel, as you open the doors.

Help me to call upon your name in all my need, and to give thanks unto you, praise you, magnify you, and sanctify your holy name, as a vessel of your mercy, forever and ever, amen.

— *John Bradford*

Set me apart, Lord

Almighty, eternal, living, and true God, you are creator of heaven and earth and men, together with your co-eternal Son, our Lord Jesus Christ, who was crucified for us and raised from the dead, and your living, pure, and true holy Spirit.

You are the wise, good, faithful, gracious and just God. The pure and faithful Savior, who gives life and law. You have said: "I have no pleasure in the death of the wicked, but that the wicked turn from his way and live" (Ezekiel 33:11). And "call upon me on the day of trouble; I will deliver you" (Psalm 50:15).

I confess that I am a poor sinner before you. I am burdened with many sins. I have broken your holy commandments in many ways, and I mourn from my heart that I have offended you. For the sake of your dear Son, our Lord and Savior Jesus Christ, who was nailed to the cross for our sakes and raised again from the dead, I pray that you would have mercy on me. Forgive me my sins, and justify me by and for the sake of the Lord Jesus. He is your eternal Word and image. Led by your wonderful and indescribable guidance, and by your inscrutable wisdom and mercy, you delivered him as a sacrifice, mediator, redeemer, and savior.

I also appeal to you: Set me apart, sanctify me by your holy, living, pure, and true Spirit. That way, I can truly acknowledge and firmly believe, obey, thank, fear, and call upon you. That way, I can behold your grace-filled appearance with joy throughout all eternity. That way, I can serve you forever.

I have hoped in you, Lord. Let me never be perplexed. Deliver me. Make me righteous, and bring me into eternal life.

You have redeemed me, God of faithfulness and truth.

Amen.

— *Philip Melanchthon*

WE ARE SO SLEEPY

Lord, we are so sleepy, so fascinated by our sins. Nothing is more difficult than to put off our own nature and renounce the wickedness we have become so used to.

Awaken us with your discipline, so we may return to you truly. Then, when our outlook is changed and we have renounced all wickedness, we may submit ourselves to you sincerely and from the heart.

Then we may look forward to the coming of your Son, cheerfully and joyfully waiting for him. Then, as we strive for this life renovation that strips us of all corruptions, we will finally be renewed in your image.

We will experience that glory obtained for us by the blood of your Son. Amen.

— *John Calvin*

FROM HEAVINESS TO JOY

Cleanse me from secret faults, Lord. And hold me back from overstepping—from those presumptuous sins—so they do not have dominion over me.

Be merciful to me for your name's sake, for my sins are great. They have taken such a hold on me that I am not able to look up. They are so numerous that my heart fails me. Deliver me, please, Lord. Hurry to help me. Increase your mercies on my account. You save those who trust in you!

Heal my soul, for I have sinned against you. I have sinned, but I am done with that, and I turn from my evil ways. I turn to my own heart, and with my whole heart and all my strength I turn to you. I seek your face and beg you.

Now from your dwelling place, Lord, and from the glorious throne of your kingdom in heaven, hear the prayer and the request of your servant, and show me your favor. Heal my soul.

O God, be merciful to me, a sinner. Be merciful to me the, chief of sinners.

Father, I have sinned against heaven, and before you. I am no longer worthy to be called your son. Treat me as one of your hired servants (Luke 15:18–19).

Make me one, or even the last, or the least among all.

What profit is there in my death, if I go down to the pit?
Will the dust praise you? Will it tell of your faithfulness?
(Psalm 30:9)

Hear, O Lord, and have mercy on me. Lord, be my helper.
Turn my heaviness into joy. Amen.

— *Lancelot Andrewes*

A PRAYER OF REMORSE FOR THE NATION

It is enough, O Lord! For never was there nation that so
horribly abused and scorned your gospel as we have done.
And we still do. You would be right if you took away our
peace, and gave it to a nation that would bring forth its fruits.

For years you have come to look for fruit, but you found
none—only leaves. Or no, you did not find leaves. For our
wickedness is now so obvious that everyone can see, to our
shame, how we only ever received the gospel to cover over our
covetousness, ambition, and crude pleasures and appetites.

Dear Father, do not cut us down yet. Let the sweet figs of
your sweet gospel remain with us. Dig around us, and lay
down fertilizer. So then we will, I trust, bring forth fruit to
the praise of your name.

Do not allow the wicked to say, "Where is their God?"
Our God is in heaven, and you may do whatever you like.
So turn us to yourself, O Lord. Save us, and continue your
gospel and faith among us. For your Son's sake, our Savior
Jesus Christ. Amen.

— *John Bradford*

I need your remedy

For the sake of your name, O Lord, forgive my iniquity, for it is great.

O dear Lord! Great and terrible God! I have sinned before you. I wandered from you, and not walked in your commands. I have rejected your grace and your holy word. I have crucified your beloved Son, I grieved your Holy Spirit, and I have acted unjustly in all my doings.

Lord, the multitude of my sins frighten me. My sins are more numerous than the sands of the seashore and the stars in the heavens. They trouble by day and night. Nothing good dwells in my flesh. All that I seek is unrighteousness and sin, and I do not know where to go. If I go into myself, I find great faults and impure desires. if I go to my neighbors, they have nothing to give me. Nothing helps, except your word.

The wages of sin, says Paul, is death. But your grace is eternal life. I seek and desire this grace, for it is the only ointment which can heal my soul.

O Lord! O dear Lord! I want your help. I seek only comfort with you, O Lord, for your holy name's sake. Help me, that I may praise you forever.

Wash me and be merciful to me in all my sins, for they are great. Amen.

— *Menno Simons*

WILL YOU FORGET ME FOREVER?

Son of David, you have found a ransom for me. Have mercy on me. Lord, help me!

Even the dogs may eat the crumbs which fall from their master's table. Have patience with me, Lord. I confess I do not have the ability to pay. Forgive me the entire debt, I beg you.

Will you forget me forever, Lord? How long will you hide your face from me? For how long can I seek answers in my own soul, and yet be so frustrated in my heart, day and night? For how long will my enemies triumph over me?

Consider and hear me, O Lord my God. Flood my eyes with light, so I will not fall asleep in death. For if you cast me down, those who trouble me will celebrate.

But my trust is in your mercy. Amen.

— *Lancelot Andrewes*

Let me dwell in your mansion, Lord

Lord, you said for us to "Come to me, all who labor and are heavy laden, and I will give you rest" (Matthew 11:28). Truly I am burdened beyond measure, and I groan under the awful weight of my sins. But I hurry to you, fountain of living water. Come unto me, Lord Jesus, so I may be able to come unto you. I am coming to you because you have first come to me. And I desire you most ardently, for I can find no good in myself at all. And if I could find anything good in me, I would not so anxiously long for you.

Truly, Lord, I dare not compare myself to any of your saints, nor even to any repentant sinner, except perhaps to the penitent thief on the cross. Have mercy on me, Lord, who showed yourself so merciful to that repentant criminal.

My life has been one of sin; but, oh! I do want to die the death of the godly and righteous. Yet godliness and righteousness are far from my heart, so I take refuge in your godliness and righteousness. You gave your life as a ransom for many; let that reassure me in my distress. You gave your most holy body to be scourged, spit upon, buffeted, lacerated with thorns, and crucified—and all for me. Let your precious blood, which you freely shed, and which cleanses us from all sin, be my help.

"While we were still sinners, Christ died for us" (Romans 5:8). Who does not wonder at this? Who is not struck with deep amazement? Unasked by anyone, even hated by men, the most merciful Son of God intercedes for sinners and for his enemies. And not only that, but you rendered a perfect satisfaction to divine justice for our sins by his poor and humble birth, his holy life, by his bitter sufferings, and by his cruel death.

O blessed Lord Jesus, who suffered and died for me before I ever showed any interest in your merit and passion, and before ever I sought you to pay the ransom for my redemption, how would you now cast me away from your face? How could you deny me the blessed fruits of your holy passion, when I cry to you for mercy out of the depths of my sin? I was your enemy by nature, but since you have died for me, I have through grace become your friend, your brother, your sister, your child. You regarded me while yet an enemy and before ever I uttered a prayer to you.

Now if I come to you, you will not cast me out, because your word is truth itself. You have spoken to us in spirit and truth, and we have received from you the words of eternal life.

Draw me closer, Lord Jesus, so I may possess that which I look for with an unwavering hope. Let me be with you as your servant, I pray, and let me behold your glory which the Father has given you. Let me someday dwell in that mansion which you have gone to prepare for me in your Father's house.

Blessed are they that dwell in your house, O Lord; they will praise you forever and ever, amen.

— *Johann Gerhard*

YOU DID NOT DIE JUST FOR ALL THE LITTLE SINS

Father of heaven, Son of God, Redeemer of the world, and Holy Spirit who proceeds from them both, three persons and one God—have mercy on me, a miserable sinner.

I have offended heaven and earth, more than my tongue can express. So where do I go, and where do I flee for relief? I am ashamed to lift up my eyes to heaven, and in earth I find no refuge.

So what do I do? Lose hope? Give up? God forbid.

O God, you are merciful. You never turn away anyone who comes to you for help. So I run to you. I humble myself before you. My sins are great, but have mercy on me for your great mercy.

You did not become a man for our small offenses. You did not give up your Son to death just for small sins, but for all and the greatest sins of the world, so sinners could return to you in their hearts—as I am doing right now.

So have mercy on me, O Lord. Although my sins are great, yet your mercy is greater.

I crave nothing, O Lord, on my own account. This is for your name's sake, to make it holy, and for the sake of your dear Son, Jesus Christ. Father in heaven, holy be your name. Your kingdom come!

Amen.

— *Thomas Cranmer*

I FLY TO YOU FOR REFUGE

I fly to you for refuge, blessed Christ, my only redeemer and savior. My sins are certainly great. But greater still is the payment you have made for them.

Great is my unrighteousness, but greater by far is your righteousness. I admit my sin. Please, in your grace, would you pay its penalty? I reveal the sin, in your mercy conceal it. With remorse I uncover it; please hide it, in your grace.

There is nothing in me but sin that deserves your condemnation. But in you there is nothing but grace that gives me a blessed hope of salvation.

I hear a voice in Scripture which tells me to hide in the clefts of the rock (Exodus 33:22). You are the rock that cannot be moved (1 Corinthians 10:4), and your wounds are those clefts. In them I will hide from the accusations of the world.

My sin cries aloud to heaven for vengeance, but still more loudly cries out your blood shed for my sins (Hebrews 12:24).

My sins accuse me before God, but your suffering is mightier for my defense. My horribly wicked life calls for my condemnation, but your holy and righteous life pleads more powerfully still for my salvation. I appeal from the throne of your justice to the throne of your mercy. I have no desire to come before your judgment—unless your holy merit intervenes between me and your sentence.

Have mercy on us, only God of mercy, and turn our stony hearts to you! Amen!

— Johann Gerhard

I AM A FRUITLESS TREE, BUT...

O holy God, righteous judge, my life terrifies me. A careful look discloses only sin and unfruitfulness, and what fruit that does appear is either so false, or imperfect, or in some way so corrupted, that it either cannot please you, or is absolutely displeasing to your eyes.

Truly, my whole life is, on the one hand, sinful and worthy of your condemnation. And on the other hand, it is unfruitful and wrecked. But why distinguish between unfruitful and worthy of condemnation? Surely if it is unfruitful it is to be condemned, for every tree that does not bring forth good fruit will be cast into the fire (Matthew 3:10). And not only will that tree be burned which bears evil fruit, but also the one that bears no fruit.

So when I think of those on your left hand in the judgment, Lord, I am horrified, since they are there not because they have done anything bad, but because they have done nothing good (Matthew 25:32). To the hungry they gave no food, and to the thirsty no drink.

How then can I possibly be saved? Who is he that is called the Wonderful, the Counselor (Isaiah 9:6)? It is Jesus Himself, the very one who is my judge, and in whose hands I am trembling with fear. So I take courage, and I despair not. I hope in him and flee to him for refuge.

O Jesus Christ, for you name's sake, deal with me according to your name. Look on me with mercy, a miserable sinner, as I call upon you. It is true, O Lord, that my participation in sin calls for condemnation, and my penitence can never satisfy you. But it is also certain that your mercy exceeds all my offense.

In you, O Lord, I put my trust, amen.

— *Johann Gerhard*

STILL WE STRUGGLE WITH OUR PRIDE

Lord, the disease of pride remains fixed in us, passed down through our original corruption from our father Adam. So teach us to subdue our spirits and to not be pleased with the way we behave. Let us recognize our lack of all wisdom and a moral compass without you.

We fly to your pity, Lord, and we confess that we are completely subject to eternal death. So may we rely on the goodness you have stooped to offer us through your gospel.

May we trust in the mediator you have given us. May we never hesitate to run to you, and to call you Father. Then, renewed by your Spirit, help us to walk in true humility and modesty, until you raise us up to your kingdom. Amen.

— *John Calvin*

Save me from the flood

Look! You are angry, Lord, because we have sinned. We are all unclean, and all our righteousness is like filthy rags. We fade like a leaf in autumn. Our iniquities, like the wind, have taken us away.

But now, Lord, you are our Father, and we are clay—the work of your hands. Do not be angry with us, and do not remember our sins forever. We are your people, Lord. See? We beg you, though our wrongdoings testify against us, and we have often slid back into sin, forgive us for the sake of your name.

You are in our midst, Lord. We are called by your name. Do not leave us. Hope of Israel, you are a savior in times of trouble. Why should you be a stranger in the land, a sojourner who is only spending the night? A mighty man who cannot save? Be merciful to our unrighteousness, and remember our iniquities no more.

Lord, I am carnal, sold into sin. No good thing dwells in me, in my flesh. For the good that I want, I do not do, but the evil I do not want is what I keep on doing. Who will deliver me from this body of death? (Romans 7)

I thank God through Jesus Christ, that where sin increased, grace abounded all the more (Romans 5:20).

O Lord, your goodness leads me to repent. Give me repentance to rescue me from the devil's snare, when I am his captive. My past life was enough to have done the will of lusts—walking in wantonness, carousing, drunkenness, and other excesses.

Lamb of God, you are spotless, and you have redeemed me by your precious blood. Have mercy on me and save me by that blood, and by your name. There is no other name by which we can be saved.

You know my foolishness, God. My faults are not hidden from you. You also know my desires and my groanings. Take me out of the mire so I do not I sink. Deliver me from those who hate me, and out of the deep waters. Do not let me drown in the flood, or be swallowed in the deep, and do not let the pit shut its mouth on me. Amen.

— *Lancelot Andrewes*

YOU PRONOUNCE ME "NOT GUILTY"

I come to you, dear Father, not by my choice nor in my own worthiness, but because of your command and promise, which cannot mislead nor deceive me.

Please forgive me, not because I can make restitution or because I merit anything by my works, but because you have promised and set your seal to the promise, making it as certain as a "not guilty" verdict spoken by yourself. Amen.

— *Martin Luther*

WE HAVE WANDERED, BUT YOU
WILL RAISE US UP

Raise us up, O blessed Jesus, from the awful death of sin, so we may walk in newness of life with you from now on.

May your death, O Christ, put to death the old Adam in us, and may your resurrection call into new life our inward being!

May your precious blood cleanse us from all our sins, and your resurrection clothe us as in a robe of righteousness!

We who have been dead in sin most ardently yearn for you, O true life.

We who have so foolishly wandered away through our sins, turn with longing hearts to you, the true and only righteousness.

Condemned to eternal death for our sins, we look with yearning hearts to you, the true salvation.

Make us alive by your Spirit! Justify us by your grace! And save us for your mercy's sake! Amen.

— Johann Gerhard

WE REMAIN HERE, FOR NOW

Father, our kingdom should not be of this world. But with sorrow we lament before you that it *is* of this world, as we testify when we offer the Lord's Prayer, "thy kingdom come."

For we are in the kingdom of the world, which is a kingdom of sin, death, and hell. But Father, help us out of this kingdom. We find ourselves in it clear over our ears, and will not be freed from it until the end. It clings to us even in death.

Lord, forgive us this evil, and help us into your kingdom! Amen.

— Balthasar Hubmaier

May we trade in our righteousness?

O Lord our God, since you have consented to instruct us in true righteousness, please let us share that righteousness by means of a true and lively faith in your Son Christ Jesus.

Do not judge us in that day according to our own righteousness, which is full of unrighteousness and uncleanness. Instead, pass by our sins and our iniquities. Accept the righteousness of your Son Christ Jesus for our unrighteousness.

Then we, clothed with his righteousness, may be included among those to whom it will be said, "Come, you who are blessed by my Father" (Matthew 25:34).

Amen.

— Henry Airay

I TRADE MY HEART OF STONE
FOR A NEW ONE

Lord, in your highness you bow your head, so now we have hope that you truly hear us. You offer your kiss of reconciliation, of your own accord. You were the one who had been grieved and wronged, yet you reached out to us who had done the wrong.

You reach out your arms to embrace us. You stretch out your nail-scarred hands to give us all things abundantly, without holding anything back. Your heart is open to receive us, if we will enter at the open door. Your feet will never leave us, if we do not leave you.

Our Father and Lord, you see the hardness of our heart—and the dullness of it. It is not enough for us to be attracted and called so gently, so sweetly, and so lovingly. You must be willing even to draw us, pull us, compel us, and drag us.

But this old heart is stony. It feels no gentleness. It is not moved with any hope of the good things you promise. So create in us a new and obedient heart.

Amen.

— *Book of Christian Prayers of 1578*

Help us to mourn

God of mercy, give us a well of blessed tears so that we, like Peter, may mourn our sins from the bottom of our hearts.

How great and grievous are those sins that burden and entangle us! But do not let us sink down in heaviness and desperation. Keep us from falling under such a heavy burden. Set us up again, and convert us thoroughly. Send the grace of your holy repentance into our heart. Wash away all our sins and negligence. Grant us the light of new graces and gifts.

Do not allow to perish those souls for whom you submitted yourself to so many pains and rebukes, and for whom you ultimately suffered the terrible bitter death of the cross. Amen.

— *Myles Coverdale*

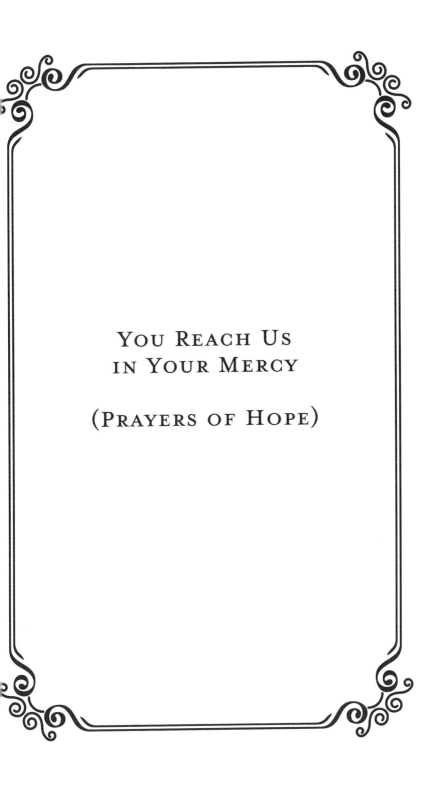

You Reach Us
in Your Mercy

(Prayers of Hope)

Please adopt me

Lord, even though I walked the wrong path since I was young, I appear now before your throne of grace. I know you are merciful and kind, and you do not want sinners to die. You want us to repent—and live!

Your prophets preached the way of repentance. So did your faithful servant, Moses. They spoke against sin and proclaimed your grace far abroad. Your sharp, piercing word was in their mouths. They taught the truth.

And you sent your beloved Son, the dear pledge of your grace. He preached your word, fulfilled your righteousness, and accomplished your will. He bore our sins, blotted them out with his blood, and brought about reconciliation. He conquered the devil, hell, sin, and death. And he obtained grace, mercy, favor, and peace for all who truly believe on him.

His command is eternal life. He sent out his messengers, ministers, and apostles of peace to spread this grace through the whole world. And they shone as bright, burning torches before all, that they might lead me and all erring sinners into the true way.

O Lord, not unto me, but unto you be praise and honor. I believe your Son, Christ Jesus, whom they preached to me. I believe! I seek his will and his way. I acknowledge your abundant, great love—not through me, but through you.

For you are good, and I am evil. You are true, and I am deceitful. You are righteous, and I am unrighteous. Teach

me the right way, dear Lord. Adopt me; I am of your
pasture. Take me into your care, under the shadow of your
wings. Protect me! Amen.

— Menno Simons

WE ARE YOUR CHILDREN ...
AND YOUR SPOUSE

Lord, you were not only pleased to adopt us as your
children, but also to unite us to yourself in a bond of
marriage, and to give us a pledge of this sacred union in
your only-begotten Son.

Now please grant that we may continue in the faith of your
gospel, and so honestly keep the pledge we gave to you.
Show yourself to us as a husband and as a father. And to
the very end, may we find in you that merciful kindness
we need to guard us in the holy fear of your name—until
in the end we enjoy fellowship with you in your heavenly
kingdom, through Christ our Lord. Amen.

— John Calvin

BE CLOSE, LORD, IN OUR MARRIAGE AND HOME

Almighty God and Father of our Lord Jesus Christ, we thank you through your dear son Jesus Christ, who has created humanity and those who are brought together as one in marriage.

We pray that you will, for your dear Son's sake, preserve us in ongoing faith in you. And next, in the faith in which we have married each other, according to your will, we pray that we may live together in peace and truth, pure and godly, giving you praise.

Give us favor and a future, protect what you have made, and protect us—that we may serve you as one, equally yoked. Protect our home and our bed by your holy angels; protect us from all impurity and immorality. May we live together in love and harmony, for your praise and our good.

Let not your enemy the devil have any entry here. Give us true peace that the world cannot give. And as we seek righteousness, our true calling, bless us with life's fruit, that we may see a harvest of children who will praise you, and then see the Christian church built up as we gather.

O Lord, live in our hearts! Never leave us! Lead us in your direction out in this world, so that when it is time to leave this life we may become, for your dear Son's sake, an everlasting kingdom and blessing, giving you honor and praise forever. Amen.

— Niels Hemmingsen

THERE BUT FOR YOUR GRACE

O merciful God, preserve our hearts from pride, conceit, and shameful covetousness. Give us grace to abide in your holy work assignment, and to be thankful for your grace. As we keep in mind how easy it is to fall, help us to walk in your fear before you.

For if we stand, we must be careful not to fall, and not look down on those who as yet do not stand.

Help us to continue in your grace, for we have nothing that we did not receive from you. And if, in weakness, we do fall, put your hand under us, Lord. Do not let us despair in sin, but cause us with repentance and sorrow for our offense to turn back to you.

Keep us from despair and from betraying your dearly beloved Son. You send him to us through your gospel. And without him we have no safeguard, but only eternal death and damnation. Keep us from that, good Lord! For your mercies' sake. Amen.

— *Myles Coverdale*

I am putting on new robes

I fear not my ignorance, Lord, for you are my wisdom. I fear not death, for you are my life. I fear not my errors, for you are my truth. I fear not my corruption, for you are my resurrection. I fear not the pains of death, for you are my joy. I fear not even the terrors of judgment, for you are my righteousness.

Let the dew of your divine grace and of your life-giving consolation be instilled into my failing soul. My spirit is drying up within me, yet soon it will rejoice in you. My flesh droops and weakens, but shortly it will spring up again into new life.

By nature, my body must undergo decay, but you will free me from decay, just as you have delivered me from every other evil. You, O God, have created me, so how can the work of your hands perish? You have delivered me from all my enemies, so how then could death alone prevail against me?

Your body, your blood, and all that you have—even your own self—you gave for my salvation. So will death then deprive me of that which was purchased with so costly a ransom?

You are my righteousness, Lord Jesus; my sins will not prevail against you. You are the resurrection and the life; death will not prevail against you. You are God; Satan will not prevail against you.

You have given me the sign of your Spirit, and in this I glory and triumph. And most firmly do I believe, doubting nothing, that I will by and by be admitted to the marriage supper of the Lamb. You, my dearest spouse, are my wedding garment, which I put on in my baptism (Galatians 3:27). You will cover all my nakedness, and I will not try to sew on to this most precious and beautiful garment the rotten tatters of my own righteousness—for what is our righteousness in your sight but filthy rags (Isaiah 64:6)? How could I dare then to patch the robe of your glorious righteousness with my own awful rags?

I will appear before your judgment seat in this robe, when you will judge the world in righteousness and equity. In this garment I will appear before you in your heavenly kingdom. This robe will so cover my confusion and shame that they will be remembered no more forever.

Then will I appear before your face glorious and holy, and this flesh of mine, this body of mine, will be clothed in your brilliant glory, a glory that continues forever and ever.

Come, Lord Jesus, come! And let whoever loves you say, come! And amen.

— *Johann Gerhard*

A PRAYER FOR FAITH, FOREVER!

Loving Savior, we are taught that whatever is not born of faith is sin (Romans 14:23), and that it is impossible to please you without faith (Hebrews 11:6). So whoever wants to come to you must believe that you are God, and that you can and will abundantly reward those who seek you in true faith.

Your eyes look on faith. You show yourself to those who have faith in you. Through faith the King of glory is married to the souls of the faithful, and you make them partakers of your divine nature through the working of your Spirit. Those who believe are justified, made children and heirs of God, and have everlasting life. By faith we receive all good things from you, even whatever we ask in your name.

Faith, then, is a precious jewel in your sight. Without it nothing is acceptable to your divine majesty.

But in our own nature we cannot own this unique treasure unless you give it to us from above, and breathe it into our hearts by your Holy Spirit. We of ourselves are blind, ignorant, and foolish, and have no way to perceive those things that pertain to the Spirit of God.

So we beg you to take away all unfaithfulness, which we received from the old Adam, and instead plant in us true faith and undoubting belief, so we are thoroughly persuaded that you are the Son of the living God, our only mediator, advocate, and intercessor. You are our only wisdom, righteousness, sanctification, and redemption. By

you alone and for your sake only, your heavenly Father is
well pleased with us. And our sins are taken away, while
grace and everlasting life are freely given to us.

Lord God, do not let us lean into our own wisdom, or
believe with blind flesh. Do not let us seek salvation
where superstitions dream. But let our faith be grounded
only on your word. And give us grace truly to believe in
you, with all our heart to put our trust in you, to look
for all good things of you, to call upon your name in
adversity, and with joyful voices and hearts praise and
magnify you in prosperity.

Do not let us doubt God the Father, nor God his Son, nor
God the Holy Spirit. But help us sincerely to believe that
you, being three distinct persons in the Deity, are yet one
very God. And beside you there is no God—neither in
heaven nor in earth.

Grant also that we may believe with assurance whatever
is written in the holy Scriptures. May we never allow
ourselves to be plucked from its truth due to any fear of
death, or the raging of this world, or the roar of the devil.

Sweet Jesus, increase this faith in us more and more
each day so that we may ultimately be made complete
and strong in faith. May we show ourselves truly faithful
before you and the world by bringing forth many good
works, to the glory and honor of your name. With God
the Father and God the Holy Spirit, you live and reign,
true God, world without end, amen.

— *Thomas Becon*

A PRAYER AT BAPTISM FOR THE GIFT OF FAITH

Almighty, eternal God and merciful Father—since the just live by faith, and since it is impossible for anyone to please you without faith, we ask that you will grant this person the gift of faith. And in this faith, would you seal and assure their heart in the Holy Spirit, according to the promise of your Son.

May the inward regeneration of the Spirit be truly represented by the outward baptism, buried with Christ into death, and raised up by him from death once again—to the praise of your glory. Amen.

— *Myles Coverdale*

SHAKE US TO LIFE

Lord, we are inclined to be fainthearted in our weakness of the flesh. Of ourselves we are unable to behold the bright shine and clearness of your glorious resurrection.

So strengthen and comfort us that we may always believe the resurrection of your Son. Through him we receive the holy hope of the life to come, and the immortal resurrection of our bodies, so that we may also comfort and strengthen others who are weak.

Cause this hard earth of our flesh to quake and move, through the power of your Spirit, to holy and fruitful repentance, change, and conversion.

Preserve us so we never resist the truth nor take part in lies. Help us to love the truth. Keep us from error and blindness.

Let our joy be in the cross of Jesus Christ your Son, and our life in his resurrection—so that we with him, and in him, may truly rise again here to a godly, righteous, and sober life, and in the world to come to the blessed life everlasting. Amen.

— Myles Coverdale

I crave the sunlight of your Spirit

Without you, O Lord, midday would be like dark night. For those unhappy souls who reject you, the sun of your grace sets and gives no light.

But in you it is never night. In you it is always clear daylight.

Our world's sun has its courses—now up, now down. But you, dear Lord, if we love you, you are always one. Always daylight.

Take this veil of sin away from me, that there might always be clear daylight in my mind!

Amen.

— John Bradford

WOULD YOU LET US KNOW YOU MORE EACH DAY?

O Lord our God, we humbly thank you for that knowledge of your Son which you have already permitted us to share.

Now we appeal to you, increase in us this knowledge daily more and more! Open our dim eyes, we beg you, so we may daily more and more see your excellence. And let us see the blessing of this knowing, so we may daily more and more grow up in all of its love.

Purge us, we ask, of all those affections or attachments that may hinder us, so that we may grow daily more and more in you, and in time may reign with you in the kingdom of your Son Christ Jesus forever, amen.

— *Henry Airay*

HELP US NEVER TO CLAIM OUR OWN RIGHTEOUSNESS

O Lord our God, open our eyes, we beg you. Help us each day to see more and more, and to behold those infinite treasures of righteousness and salvation which are laid up for us in your Son Christ Jesus!

As you have granted to make him righteousness and salvation for us, so also give us a heart to acknowledge him as our complete righteousness—the one source of our salvation.

Help us to renounce all righteousness by works of our own, so that we may daily, more and more, grow up in your Son. And then in that last and great day we may be found in him, amen!

— Henry Airay

A PRAYER FOR TRUE HUMILITY

What do we have, heavenly Father, that we have not received from you?

Every good gift and every perfect gift is from above, coming down from the Father of lights (James 1:17).

And because everything we have is yours—whether for body or soul—how can we be proud, boasting about things that are not even our own? And as you give, so you are also able to take away again. And you will, when your gifts are abused, won't you? If we fail to acknowledge that you are the giver?

So take away all my arrogance and pride. Instead, graft in true humility, so I may know that you are the giver of all good things, and be thankful for them, and use them for your glory and the good of my neighbor.

Grant also that I may not glory in earthly creatures, but in you alone. You bring mercy, equity, and righteousness on the earth, and to you alone be all glory, amen.

— Thomas Becon

Heal the pride in our hearts

O blessed Christ, graciously heal the swelling pride of our hearts. May we rest our hopes of eternal life on the merit of your holy humility! May that humility be the pattern of our lives. May our faith more firmly lay hold of your humility, and our lives be ever fashioned after your lowly life! Amen.

— Johann Gerhard

We will wait for true happiness

Almighty God, though we are constantly tossed about by various trials, and Satan always tries to shake our faith, help us still to stand firm on the promise you gave us: that you will forever encourage and offer us hope. You will always be our reconciler.

You have confirmed this promise in your Son, so we will not despair—even in our greatest troubles. We may come to you, relying on your goodness, until our time of deliverance ripens fully.

Meanwhile, help us not to envy the fleeting happiness of your enemies. Instead, help us to wait patiently, while you show that our chief desire is your encouragement and support. And for those who provoke and anger you, even every good thing they receive is cursed, until Christ at last reveals to us the real happiness and glory of your church, when he appears at the last day for our salvation, amen.

— John Calvin

Help us to appreciate your gifts, without envy

Lord, you are the inventor and maker of all things, the giver of gifts in your abundant generosity. You give to each of us more than we deserve—enough to each person. So we have no cause for resentment or envy.

Grant that we would not envy, but remain quietly content. Help us to be thankful for what we receive, and never to murmur against the way you decide to distribute your free benefits.

Rather, may we love and praise your abundant generosity in our life and in the lives of others. And may we always magnify you, Lord. You are the deep well of all gifts and goodness. To you be glory forever, amen.

— *Primer of 1559*

May we mourn that our sins pierced your side

Lord, give us grace when we look to the death and passion of Christ, that we may get a sense of our own misery. May we be in sadness and mourn that our sins pierced the sides of the innocent—the God of glory, even! And help us to know that we may have recourse to this suffering, and to get grace in our Lord. To whom, with the Father, and the Holy Spirit, be all honor, praise, and glory, forever and ever. Amen.

— *Robert Rollock*

Help me to pass along your gifts

I give you thanks, O God almighty, because you have not only given me the gifts of nature—reason, power, and strength—but because you have also given me the substance of this world, and plentifully.

Lord, I know that these are your gifts. You give these gifts freely.

I know also with the prophet Haggai that the silver is yours, and the gold is yours (Haggai 2:8). You give it to whomever you please. To the godly, that they may dispose and distribute your gifts. And to the ungodly, it only adds to their condemnation.

So God of mercy, I humbly ask that you with your Holy Spirit would build in me a faithful heart and a ready hand to distribute your gifts according to your will and pleasure. As an example to those who are humble and weak, and for your glory, may I not keep things for my own comfort. And may I not store these things up here, where thieves may steal and moths ruin, but instead seek treasure in your heavenly kingdom, far from thieves and moths. In your mercy you have promised your own reward.

To you be all honor and praise, with the Son and the Holy Spirit. Amen.

— Primer of 1559

Keep us humble

Lord, it is tough for us to live a prosperous life without the danger of warping our minds in the process. So help us to remember our own mortality. May our frailty be ever so obvious to our eyes. May it make us humble and lead us to give you all the glory.

With you as our advisor, teach us to walk with care and respect of others. May we submit ourselves to you, and conduct ourselves with modesty among the people around us.

May we also never despise or insult our fellow believers, but always aim to live and work with moderation as our goal … until at last you gather us into the glory that was bought for us by the blood of Jesus. Amen.

— John Calvin

Help us to keep the right treasure

Lord grant that every one of us may print these sayings on our heart, and put into practice this holy work: So direct us in your ways, that even as we get and use transitory, earthly goods, we lose not the everlasting treasure of your heavenly kingdom.

We give you heartfelt thanks, God our redeemer, and humbly plead with you to keep and increase us in the true faith, and lastly to bring us to life everlasting. Amen.

— Heinrich Bullinger

A PRAYER FOR COMPASSION
ON MY WAY TO WORK

Merciful Father and Savior, in your grace I ask you to bless my labor. I cannot go on without your blessing. May it be a witness of your bounty and support, and by it may we come to know the fatherly care you have for us.

I pray also that you would strengthen me by your Holy Spirit, that I may work without fraud or deceit. Help me to follow your way—rather than seek to satisfy greedy affections or desire for gain.

Lord, if it pleases you to prosper my labor, give me a mind also to help those in need, according to whatever ability you in your mercy give me. And knowing that all good things are from you, grant that I may humble myself to my neighbor, and not by any means lift myself above anyone who has not received as much as I.

If it pleases you to train me through greater poverty and need than my flesh would desire, yet would you please grant me grace to know that you will continue to nourish me in your generosity. Then I will not be tempted and fall into distrust, but patiently wait until you fill me not only with graces and benefits here on earth, but with your heavenly and spiritual treasures. Then I may always have plenty of opportunities to give you thanks, and to wholly rest on your mercies.

Hear me, Lord of mercy, through Jesus Christ your Son our Lord. Amen.

— John Knox

Help us to look first
to our neighbors

Merciful Father in heaven, give us your grace and help to love our neighbors from the heart, and to always do them good—both in words and deeds. Grant that we may live purely, avoiding offense to others, and provoking no one to unclean living. Help us to encourage others to honesty.

May we help others to save and keep what they have. And if they live in poverty, help us to relieve them as we are able.

May we never hurt others with a false witness, but instead always speak well of our neighbor.

Keep us from evil lusts and desires, never wanting what belongs to others.

For this is your will, and you have commanded us to be obedient.

Amen.

— *Thomas Cranmer*

Let me fly to you in prayer

Lord, give us more grace to do as you command, and then command us however you will.

So often as we hear or read your promises and your warnings, may we recognize and confess our own defiance and disobedience. As we see how it is not in us to bend to you unless you touch us with your Holy Spirit, let us fly to you and pray:

Lord, take from me my hard and stony heart, and give me instead a soft and fleshy one. May your promises and warnings work in me to bring obedience to your will.

So often as I hear or read of your admonitions or exhortation, let me take them to heart, acknowledging my own shortcomings. And seeing how I cannot myself will or do what you urge me to do, let me fly to you in prayer.

Lord, frame my will according to your blessed will, that I may do what your will is! I cannot run the race the Scriptures urge me to run, but you must work in me both the will and the doing.

Lord, sanctify and purify me with your Holy Spirit. Then, by your guiding grace, I will walk in those good works which you have ordained for me until life's end. Amen.

— *Henry Airay*

I DO NOT MEASURE UP

Our righteousness, Lord, however excellent it seems to us, compared with yours, is nothing but unrighteousness.

A lamp that gleams in the darkness is overshadowed in the light of the sun. Often a stick is supposed to be straight until compared with a ruler, and its crookedness appears.

And so often a deed that glows in the opinion of the doer appears as nothing in view of the judge. The judgments of people are one thing, the judgments of God something else.

Just bringing to mind my many sins terrifies me. But oh! How many more escape my memory!

"Who can discern his errors? Declare me innocent from hidden faults" (Psalm 19:12). Amen.

— Johann Gerhard

FROM PASSION COMES LIFE AND GLORY

Lord, we are all sinners, living under sin and death. We strive to be found in Jesus, that by faith in him we may find his passion—his suffering and sacrifice. And we desire that passion's powerful and abundant result: to free and deliver us from the bonds of sin and death, and so be made partakers of life and glory through him, to whom with the Father and the Holy Spirit be all honor, praise, and glory. Amen.

— Robert Rollock

I welcome the new me

See, Lord Jesus, how poorly I have treated your suffering? My heart is deeply pained and my soul greatly saddened, because I have no works or merits of my own to offer for my salvation. Yet since your suffering, Jesus, may be my work, let your works also be my merit.

Surely I do not treat your suffering the right way. Because even though it is surely enough for my salvation, I try to supplement it by my own good works. And if I should discover any righteousness in myself, your righteousness would be of no use to me, or certainly I should not so ardently desire it.

If I seek to justify myself by the deeds of the law, I will be condemned by the law. I know that I am no longer under the law, but under grace (Romans 6:14).

I have lived shamefully. "Father, I have sinned against heaven and before you. I am no longer worthy to be called your son" (Luke 15:21). But do not refuse to call me your servant. I appeal to you, do not deny me the wonderful benefits of your suffering. May your precious blood yet free me from my sin. Sin has always lived in me; I beg you, now, let it die with me.

Up to now the flesh has dominated me; now let the Spirit triumph in me. Let the outward person perish, so the inward person may rise into new glory. Up to now I have always followed the temptations of the devil. I pray that you would now let him be trampled under my feet (Romans 16:20).

Satan is at hand to accuse me, but he has nothing in me.
The very idea of death terrifies me, and yet death will
mark the end of my sins and the beginning of a perfectly
holy life. Then at last I will be able to please you perfectly,
O my God. Then at last I will be established in goodness
and virtue. Amen.

— *Johann Gerhard*

THERE IS NO OTHER HOPE

Father of mercy, we cry to you in all trouble, and we call
on you through the crucified Jesus.

Do not let us sink in great distress, and do not give us over
to our own strength. As much as the enemy presses in on
us, help us even more.

For in all anguish and trouble you are our helper and
most faithful friend. If, in your fatherly will, you allow
temptation to come on us, grant us grace to patiently bear
it. Grant us grace to lay the burden upon your mercy.
There is no other hope. So in every trouble may we put
our whole trust in you alone. Amen.

— *Myles Coverdale*

Keep us from hardening our hearts

Lord, allow no temptation to fall upon us that is greater than your help in us. Be stronger in us than any temptation that comes upon us.

Though we are negligent, unthankful, and disobedient— even so, do not let the devil loose upon us to deceive us with his false prophets. Do not allow us to be hardened, as you did Pharaoh, with the false miracles of his sorcerers.

A little wind drives a great ship, Lord, and a little miracle can confirm and harden someone in their opinions—what their blind reason already believes. A few false miracles were enough to persuade Pharaoh in his greediness to hold the children of Israel in bondage. He believed the true miracles Moses showed him were not of you ... and his heart hardened.

So a little thing is enough to make those who do not walk in your truth (and so are unable to understand your Son's doctrine) believe superstition and become hardened. Blind human nature delights in evil and is ready to believe lies.

Our corrupt nature can only fall downward, Lord.
The devil and the world would drive it down the same direction. How can we move higher and stand in virtue if your power ceases in us? So do not lead us into temptation, merciful Father, and may you never stop governing us.

Amen.

— *William Tyndale*

GRANT ME THE POWER TO DO

All the glory of the godly is in the shame of our Lord's suffering. All our rest is in the wounds of our crucified Savior. His death is our life; his exaltation is our glory.

How great is your mercy, O heavenly Father and almighty God! By my own power have I offended you, but by my own power has it been impossible to please you. So you in Christ are reconciling me to yourself.

See, O holy God, the sacred mystery of your flesh, and dismiss the guilt of my flesh. Graciously regard what your blessed Son has patiently suffered, and overlook what your sinful servant has done. My flesh has provoked you to anger, but let the flesh of your Son, I pray, incline you to mercy.

My sins deserve the severest punishment at your hands, but far more has the devotion of my Redeemer merited your mercy. Great is my unrighteousness, but greater far is the righteousness of my Redeemer. As far as the mighty God is above puny humans, so far is my wickedness beneath his goodness, in quality as well as in quantity.

All that I am is yours, because you have created me. Grant, O Lord, that it may be wholly yours also by free and happy choice. You lead me to ask (Matthew 7:7), so grant that I may also receive! You enable me to seek; grant that I may find. You teach me to knock; open unto me, I pray, when I do knock. The desire comes from you; may the power to obtain come also from you. From you I have the power to will; grant me also the power to do (Philippians 2:13). Amen.

— *Johann Gerhard*

WE DID NOT DESERVE THIS

Remember, O Lord, your compassion and loving devotion, for they are from age to age.

O Lord of hosts, when I am buoyed up in the waters of your grace, I cannot fathom or measure them. Your mercies are greater than all your works.

Who did you ever reject that came to you with a devoted heart? Who sought you and did not find you? Who desired your help, or prayed for your grace, and did not receive it? And who called to you that you did not hear?

How many have you accepted in grace, who, according to your strict justice, deserved something else?

Adam turned away from you and believed the serpent. He broke your covenant to become a child of death. But your fatherly kindness did not reject him. You sought him in grace. You called him, corrected him, and covered him.

Paul, your chosen vessel, raved like a roaring lion. But your grace shone around him in his blindness and illuminated him. You called him and chose him as an apostle and servant.

And me, dear Lord—your fatherly grace did not forsake me, a wretched sinner. You received me in love, converted me to another mind, led me by the hand, and taught me by your Holy Spirit.

Your mercies are greater than all your works. So help
me, dear Lord. Stand by me and comfort me. My soul
is in great distress, and the dangers of hell surround me.
Preserve me and do not be angry. Remember your great
and tender mercies, Lord, and your lovingkindness. Amen.

— *Menno Simons*

THERE IS ONLY ONE CURE

Lord, as you urge us daily to repentance, and we are
stung with the consciousness of our own sins, help us
not to grow stupid in our vices or deceive ourselves with
empty flattery.

Instead, help us to carefully examine our own life, and
then together confess that we are all guilty—not just of
light offenses, but of offenses that deserve eternal death.

And no other cure remains for us ... except your infinite
mercy. So we seek a share of that grace which has been
once offered to us by your Son, and is daily offered to
us by his gospel. By relying on him as our mediator, we
entertain hope even in the midst of a thousand deaths,
until we are gathered into that blessed life bought for us by
the blood of your only Son. Amen.

— *John Calvin*

We are your flock—I come to you

Lord, you are the God and father of my life! Hear me. In all my troubles and miseries, I fly to you alone.

You, O Lord, are the only defender and deliverer of those who put their trust in you. And I come to you, merciful Savior, craving your mercy and help.

It makes sense that we should be visited some time with some adversity, so we might be tested to see if we are of your flock, and so we may come to know ourselves and you better. Yet you said you would not allow us to be tried beyond our power. So be merciful to me, I pray.

With Solomon, I cry to you: May I neither be too puffed up with prosperity, nor too much depressed with adversity. Otherwise if I were too full, I might deny you. Or brought too low, I might despair and blaspheme you, my Lord and Savior (Proverbs 30:8–9).

Merciful Savior, you know my misery best. Be now my strong tower of defense. Allow me now to not be tried beyond my strength. Either deliver me out of this great misery, or else give me the grace to patiently bear your heavy hand and sharp correction.

Your right hand delivered the people of Israel out of the hands of Pharaoh, who oppressed them four hundred years. In your fatherly goodness deliver me now, a person for whom your son Christ shed his precious blood on the cross.

How long will you be absent? Forever? Oh, Lord! In your displeasure have you forgotten to be gracious, and have you shut up your lovingkindness? May we come to you with our requests no longer? Is your mercy clearly gone forever, and has your promise come utterly to an end?

Why do you delay so long? Shall I despair of your mercy? Oh God! Far be that from me. I am your workmanship, created in Christ Jesus. Give me grace therefore to patiently bear your works, knowing with assurance that as you can, so you will deliver me—when it pleases you. I do not doubt or mistrust your goodness toward me, for you know better what is good for me than I do.

So do with me in all things what you will, and plague me however you will. Only, in the meantime, I pray that you would arm me with your armor, that I may stand fast in truth. Place on me the breastplate of righteousness, and shoes prepared by the gospel of peace.

Above all things, give me the shield of faith, with which I may be able to quench all the fiery darts of the wicked. And with the helmet of salvation and the sword of your spirit, which is your most holy word, I will pray always that I may dedicate myself wholly to your will, continuing in your pleasure and comforting myself in those troubles that you are pleased to send me. Such troubles will be profitable for me, and I am persuaded that everything you do can only be well.

Hear me, merciful Father, for the sake of he who was a sacrifice for my sins, and to whom with you and the Holy Spirit be all honor and glory. Amen!

— *Lady Jane Grey*

Mercy upon mercy flows from you

Oh merciful and tender God the Father—I thank you
through your dear Son Jesus Christ, my only Savior and
blessing, that you have not condemned me for my many
large and blatant sins, according to your righteous justice.
Instead, you have graciously spared me and called me to
know your Son, Jesus Christ.

I know and believe that he is the one who blesses me, as
he blesses all those who believe in him. This is wholly
your doing that you have established in mercy.

Grant me your Holy Spirit, forgive my sins, and build my
faith, so that I may praise and honor you all my days. Oh
Lord, establish in my heart the pure and clean knowledge
of your blessed gospel. Anchor my faith and form it daily
with your Holy Spirit in me so I may honor your holy will
with a good conscience.

Do not let me wander from your pure and clear gospel
toward the devil's and the world's teaching. Do not let me
act against a clear conscience. I know the danger, Lord.
My enemies are many and fierce who would lead me away
from you. The devil never rests, the world looms, and my
own flesh and blood can never rest. These enemies follow
hard after me and would turn me away from you; they are
too strong!

So I beg you, tender Father, uphold me through your
Word and the Holy Spirit in one strong faith and in a
God-fearing life. With this I may overcome my enemies,

in your strength and through your dear Son, my Savior
Jesus Christ.

Let me always be your Son's hands and feet, sheltered
behind his shield against the devil—not just protection for
himself, but also for me, who trusts in him.

O Lord help! Help my faith. Protect me in your hand.
Lead me in your way. Rule me through your Holy Spirit.
When I face off against your enemies, give me grace to
always see the victory, and for my enemies to never see
the upper hand. And when you call me from this world,
affirm my soul with gladness in your dear Son Jesus
Christ—my only Savior and my hand of blessing.

I praise, honor, and thank you forever, tender Father,
with your Son Jesus Christ and the Holy Spirit, who is
our ever-almighty and merciful God. All the angels and
people everywhere will praise and thank you forever for
your mercy. You have proven this to me and to all helpless
sinners who come to you.

Dear Father, you command me. I place my blessings in
your hand and await the everlasting life and joy that you
have promised me in Jesus Christ my dear Savior.

Mercy upon mercy. Amen and amen.

— Niels Hemmingsen

I pray to you in my troubles

Merciful Redeemer, you are always full of compassion.
You are always our preserver, whether you send us
adversity or prosperity.

Great is your mercy and compassion. You heal us inwardly
by outward afflictions, by bitter medicine. And you
prepare us for everlasting joys by using earthly troubles.
And as you yourself have traced out the true way to joy
with your own footsteps, grant that I may patiently and
obediently drink the cup that you give me.

These challenges to me are serious, but you have suffered
much more grievous things for me. And I have deserved
far worse—even hell.

Yet you know how frail we humans are. So, like the good
Samaritan, you pour wine into our wounds, which makes
our sins sting! Yet you alleviate the pain with the oil of
your comfort, so we can endure those things which would
otherwise be intolerable.

If you think it best to increase our griefs, then increase
in me the gift of your patience. And grant also that these
afflictions would cause me to turn from my sins.

Or if in your fatherly lovingkindness you think this is
enough chastising, let this storm pass into calm weather.
Then I will thank you for correcting your unprofitable
servant in gentleness, and for putting away the bitterness
of my affliction by the sweetness of your comfort. In one

way you had necessity in mind, and in the other you remembered my weaknesses.

So to you be praise and thanks forever. Amen.

— *Book of Christian Prayers of 1578*

WE WANT TO BE THAT PECULIAR PEOPLE

Almighty God, help us not to provoke your wrath with our combativeness. But whenever you warn us, may we instantly fear and tremble at your word, and then obey you in a true spirit of meekness. May we dread your warnings in true repentance, anticipating your judgment, and so aspire to glorify your name.

May you become our strength and glory. And before the world, before you and the angels, before glory—may we demonstrate how we are that peculiar people that you have favored with your adoption, and that you may to the end carry on in us the work of your grace, through Jesus Christ our Lord. Amen.

— *John Calvin*

WE TURN FROM THE WORLD;
TURN US TO YOU

Lord Jesus! Turn us to you, and we will be turned. Heal us, and we will be holy, for without grace and help from you, no one can be truly turned or healed.

Those who turn to you today but turn away tomorrow— they only despise you. Today they might do penance, but tomorrow they are turning again to their former evils.

What is turning to God? Nothing but turning from the world, from sin, and from the devil.

What is turning from God? Nothing but turning to the changeable goods of this world, to works of the devil, and to lusts of the flesh.

To be turned from the world is to consider as nothing and to put out of mind every worldly pleasure, and then to endure meekly all its bitterness, slander, and deceits—for the love of Christ. Turning from the world means leaving behind all lawless pursuits, things that never profit the soul. Turning from the world means dying to everything the world worships and loves.

Turn us to you, Lord Jesus.

Amen.

—John Wycliffe

LET US REMEMBER YOU AND PUT ASIDE THE WORLD

Lord, strip the vain, evil clothing of pride and brutality from us. We have willingly taken it on ourselves, while you, the King of heaven, were scornfully despised in a fool's coat. So let us see clearly the contempt and derision they showed you. Teach us to follow you and rejoice when we also are despised.

But let us never set our hope on other people, or on praise, honor, power, or money. Instead, help us to truly set aside the temporary things of this world, and in love to steadfastly follow after you, our only welfare. As we taste the rebuke and contempt which you suffered for us, poor unworthy sinners, may we also in our hearts never forget what you have done. Amen.

— *Myles Coverdale*

CLOTHE US FOR THE WEDDING

O Lord, we do not want to appear before you naked. Clothe us with your wedding garment of faith and love. And when we suffer wrong against us, give us grace to follow your example in patience, so that no sorrow nor heaviness for loss of worldly goods will lead us away from you. Amen.

— *Myles Coverdale*

HELP US TO NAIL OUR SINS
ON YOUR CROSS

Grant unto us, O Lord Jesus, that neither threats nor slander would drive us away from the scorned cross, but that with all our strength we would gladly follow you.

Give us grace to nail our flesh and its temptations to the cross. Then, as we mourn our former sins, may we overcome the temptations that are behind us.

Grant us your refuge and sure defense under the shadow of your wings, and under the unstoppable power of your holy cross.

Help us, Lord, in this conflict of the spirit. Let your cross be the cure against all corruption. Grant that we would always cheerfully take up our cross and follow you. Amen.

— *Myles Coverdale*

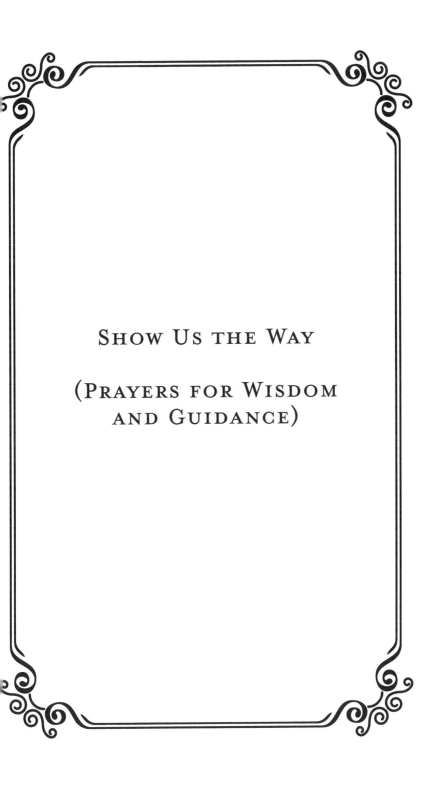

Show Us the Way

(Prayers for Wisdom and Guidance)

Help us to listen!

Lord, your word is a lamp to my feet and a light to my path (Psalm 119:105). It shows us where to walk, not to the right or the left, but the way you have appointed, to live and please you.

Your law is perfect and undefiled. It turns souls and gives wisdom—even to infants. Your ways are right, and cause the heart to rejoice.

Your commands are pure, and give light to our eyes. Your word heals all. Through the word you have left for us, we are made clean. It is the power of God for salvation to everyone who believes (Romans 1:16). It is sweeter than honey and more precious than gold.

May your preacher now teach nothing but your pure word and the glorious gospel of your Son. And may we note with diligence and keep in our memory whatever is truly spoken about the Lord.

And since neither he who plants nor he who waters is anything, but only God who gives the growth (1 Corinthians 3:7), we pray that the seed of your word planted here will fall into good ground in our hearts. May it not be choked by thorns, dried up for lack of moisture, or carried off by birds.

But through the working of the Holy Spirit may it take root in our hearts and bring forth plenty of good fruit, for your glory and the health of our souls, amen.

— *Thomas Becon*

Open our eyes to the light

O merciful, gracious Lord, enlighten the eyes of all who are blind, that they may see your heavenly brightness and confess the majesty of your honor.

May the true heavenly light, Jesus Christ, be eternally blessed.

Enlighten every dark, unschooled heart with your eternal truth and the clear and brilliant ray of your Holy Spirit. May they view the eternal brightness of Christ in sincere, pure faith to the praise and honor of his great name, and to the salvation of many souls.

Your word remains invincible and firm: "The word became flesh" (John 1:14).

Grant also that the wrathful dragon may not entirely devour your poor little flock, but that we, by your grace, may in patience conquer by the sword of your mouth. And may we plant a seed that lives on—people who keep your commandments, preserve your testimony, and eternally praise your great and glorious name.

Amen, dear Lord, amen.

— Menno Simons

Give us faithful fishers

God of mercy, help us to cling to you and follow your commands. Tame our bodies in honest labor, so we escape the pull of bad habits.

Draw our hearts always upward, so we set aside all worldly things and focus only on you.
Gracious Father, give us faithful fishers, true and careful in their calling. With the net of your holy word, may they draw us out of the raging sea, so that we with them, and they with us, may enjoy the everlasting banquet. Amen.

— *Myles Coverdale*

A prayer before I dare to preach

Open my eyes, Lord, so that I might see the wondrous things of your word. Take away the veil from my heart when I read the Scriptures.

You are blessed, O Lord. Teach me your commands. Word of the Father, give me your word. Touch my heart and enlighten the eyes of my understanding. Open my lips and fill them with your praise.

Lord, live in my heart and in my mouth, that I may set forth your truth the right way, by the sanctifying power of your most Holy Spirit.

Glowing coal, when you touched the lips of the prophet, you purified him from sin. I am a sinner; touch my lips and set me free from every stain. Make me fit to deliver your truth.

O Lord, open my lips, and my mouth will show forth your praise. Give me the tongue of the well-trained, that I may know what I ought to say.

And if there is any word good for building up, give it, that you may minister grace to the hearers.

Grant that I may speak boldly.

I open my mouth wide, O Lord. Please fill it. Amen.

— Lancelot Andrewes

BRING US GOOD JUDGES

Lord, you are the most righteous judge.

Send us judges who love truth, and hate covetousness. Judges who admit no false accusations, and who treat all equally. Judges who desire no bribes, and who hear all matters indifferently. Judges who rule with equity and justice, who deliver the oppressed from the power of the violent, who are favorable to the stranger, who defend the fatherless and the widow, who consider the cause of the righteous, who help the poor, who advance virtue, and who suppress vice.

Give us judges who behave as if they were ready right now to appear before the righteous throne of your majesty.

Grant this, merciful Father, for your dear Son's sake, Jesus Christ our Lord. Amen.

— Thomas Becon

Help us find our true north

Almighty God, every perfect gift comes from you. And some people excel in intellect or talent. But no one has anything of their own—only what you decide to give us, a measure of your gracious generosity.

Now may we apply whatever intelligence you grant us to the glory of your name. May we also acknowledge in humility and modesty that what you have committed to our care ... really belongs to you.

Restrain us in a sober frame of mind to avoid excess. Help us to remain in that simplicity of life to which you call us.

And may we not rest in earthly things, but rather learn to raise our minds to true wisdom, to acknowledge you as true God, and to devote ourselves to the obedience of your righteousness.

May this be our sole object: to devote ourselves entirely to the glory of your name throughout our lives, through Jesus Christ our Lord. Amen.

—John Calvin

As we make our way through darkness

Lord, we live in thick darkness, surrounded by so much darkness of ignorance. We often doubt your care and provision, and we imagine you have forsaken us when we do not see instant answers to prayer.

So help us now to raise our minds and not to doubt, but to remember that you look upon us. Help us to know that you command your angels to care for us. Raise us up in their hands.

Guide us in all our ways—even in all the crooked, winding roads of this life. Teach us to commit ourselves wholly to your rule, and so allow ourselves to be drawn and turned as we follow the way you have pointed out to us.

Help us to continue straight toward the mark which you have set before us, until we are ultimately gathered into your eternal rest. Amen.

— John Calvin

A PRAYER FOR SPIRITUAL LIGHT

Lord, when we see light on all sides at noontime, help our minds also to be surrounded in light.

As the sun is now clear and bright, so will our bodies be on the day of judgment.

And as the sun comes to its height in the sky, but afterwards slides down to the horizon and sets, so there is nothing in the world that is so perfect or glorious that it will not decrease when it is at its full—and so fade away.

Father, you give so much physical light; give us also spiritual light.

Amen.

— John Bradford

The portrait became clear in your word

O dear Lord, I never knew myself until I viewed myself through the lens of your word. Then I learned to recognize my blindness, nakedness, uncleanness, and depraved nature.

I learned that nothing good lived in my flesh. I was full of wounds, bruises, and awful sores from head to foot. How pitiful! My gold was worthless; my wheat was debris. My work was deceit and lies.

I walked before you in the flesh. My thoughts were carnal, my words and works utterly lacked the fear of God, and my prayers were full of hypocrisy.

In short, I did nothing without sin.

O Lord, remember not the many sins of my youth (whether they were knowing or unknowing), nor my daily transgressions, of which I am guilty in my great weakness. Instead, remember me now according to your great goodness.

I am blind; enlighten me. I am naked; clothe me. I am wounded; heal me. I am dead; raise me up.

I know of no light, medicine, or life but you. Accept me graciously. Grant me your mercy, your favor and faith, your fullness, and your good will, O Lord. Amen.

— *Menno Simons*

Spirit, lead us

Almighty God, as you shine on us by your word and show us the way of salvation, we may with open eyes look on that light. And as we are blind also at midday, open our eyes!

May the inward light of your Spirit lead us to the light of your word. Help us to never doubt that you alone are sufficient to supply us with all things necessary for enjoying life with you. Distill and refresh us so the light of faith once kindled in our hearts by your grace may never be extinguished—until we attain to the fullness which has been laid up for us in heaven.

May we now in part be satisfied with the measure of knowledge you have given us, until at last we see you face to face. And so transformed to your image, we may enjoy the fullness of that glory into which Christ our Lord has been received. Amen.

— *John Calvin*

Help me to keep learning

Lord God, Heavenly Father, because you have created us to be thoughtful creatures, people who learn and do good, so strengthen your Holy Spirit within me to always learn and do good, and thereby sanctify and magnify your name and serve my neighbors for their salvation, through our Lord Jesus Christ, amen.

— *Martin Bucer*

Show me your way, the only way

Show me your ways, O Lord. Teach me your paths.

Lord of hosts, I know through the word of your grace that there is only one way that leads to life. One straight and narrow way, found by few—and still fewer walk in that way.

That way is like a treasure hid in a field which none can find, except those who are shown by the Spirit.

Dear Lord, there is no way but you alone. Everyone who walks through you will find the gates of life.

There is another way which seems very pleasant to the flesh. It appears soft, smooth, and broad. A path with roses, agreeable to the eye. But it only leads to death.

The whole world walks this way, unconcerned and fearless. The whole world prefers perishable to imperishable, evil to good, and darkness to the light of the world. They all walk on the perverse, broad, and crooked way. They do not know the Lord's way.

True, the way of error seems right in the eyes of fools. But I know through your Spirit and your word that it is the certain road to the abyss of hell.

So I beg you, dear Lord, be merciful to me, a poor sinner. Show me your path, and teach me your way. Your way is the right way. It is godly, pleasant, humble, chaste, full of peace and of all good. And your way will lead my soul to eternal life. Amen.

— *Menno Simons*

A PRAYER FOR FINDING
THAT RIGHT SOMEONE

O almighty wise and good God, you have created me in your own image so that I may honor and praise you in this world and forevermore.

I pray for your dear Son's, my only savior Jesus Christ's sake, that you would reign over me in the Holy Spirit—and that if it would honor you, if it be your holy will, that I would honor and praise you in married life. Give me that person to live with in marriage, the one you find is right and most helpful for me.

O Lord, if it is your will, then turn my heart to this person who, in all godliness and honesty, would live with me. And never let me in my own flesh or blind passion be seduced into being unloving or hurtful.

O Lord, give me the best counsel and I give you praise, amen.

— Niels Hemmingsen

YOU ARE THE ONLY ONE
WHO KNOWS THE WAY

Lord, the beginning of the fall of man was trust in himself. And the beginning of the restoring of man was distrust in himself, and trust in God.

Our Savior, you lead those who truly trust and commit to you on the right path to immortal blessing. You are the gracious and most wise guide.

But since we are blind and feeble, grant that we may always keep you before our eyes, to follow you as our guide. Help us in obedience to be ready when you call, and to commit ourselves wholly to you. Then you— the only one who knows the way—will lead us to our heavenly desires.

Along with the Father and Holy Spirit, to you be glory forever, amen.

— *Primer of 1559*

IN SEARCH OF PURPOSE

Lord, how the world captivates and beguiles our feeble, dim eyes. All those glittering things seem great and so worth having, when in reality they are only small, empty, and to be despised.

The world calls, allures, entices, and flatters. And if that does not work, it frightens, threatens, and aggravates.

O most bright light of God's truth, scatter and chase away at once these misty clouds. Enlighten our minds so we avoid any things that are against you. (They are also harmful to us.) Help us to only seek those things that are substantial, great, and beautiful. In fact, you: the only eternal source of goodness and blessings.

All flesh is like grass, and all its glory like a flower in the field. The grass withers, and the flower fades when you breathe on it (Isaiah 40:6).

Things fly away so soon, leaving behind no fruit, and nothing but weariness and grief. Not that God created it that way, but we in our foolishness have made it so.

So deliver us from vanity and pride, Lord. Help us instead to seek your truth, to set our whole minds on your righteousness, and to discover joy in nothing but you and in your Son, Jesus Christ our Lord. Amen.

— *Book of Christian Prayers of 1578*

Deliver us from fake religion

Living, true, and everlasting God, who will and ought only and alone to be worshiped, called upon, and feared: May you give to us all a true faith, and deliver us from all vain superstition, through Jesus Christ our Lord, amen.

— *Heinrich Bullinger*

May I truly understand your word

Lord, you alone are the author of the holy Scriptures. And no matter how wise or educated, no one can understand them unless taught by your Holy Spirit—who alone is the schoolmaster to lead the faithful into all truth.

So I humbly ask that you would breathe your blessed Spirit into my heart. Renew the senses of my mind, open my wits, and reveal to me a true understanding of your holy mysteries. Plant in me such a certain and unshakeable knowledge, so that no subtle persuasion of human wisdom may pluck me from your truth. As I learn true understanding of your will, so I may always remain in it—come life or death, to the glory of your name. Amen.

— Thomas Becon

Help us to know (and live) the difference

Almighty Father, grant us a true understanding and clear vision to judge rightly in all things, through your blessed Son Jesus Christ. Help us to distinguish between holy and unholy, good and evil, right and wrong, clean and unclean—according to the truth of your good news.

For all those who have renounced gain, honor, and fame for the sake of the gospel, teach us by the sure and true confession of Scripture. May we be driven by the Holy Spirit. And may we enter into all godly wisdom, truth, righteousness, and obedience to you who have taught us by your powerful word, drawn us by your Spirit, and bought and delivered us by your precious blood.

In Christ Jesus, amen.

— *Menno Simons*

MAY WE SEE HOW FAR WE FELL

May God the Father of our Lord Jesus Christ, by the power of his Holy Spirit, so illuminate and so move our hearts that we may see clearly—and understand perfectly—how horrible has been our fall from his truth, how fearful and terrible it is to fall into his hands without hope of mercy, and what is his unspeakable mercy which yet again he offers to us.

May it please his eternal goodness to fill us with such wisdom, prudence, and determination so that we may follow his will as we see it revealed in his word. And may it be to the advancement of his glory, the consolation of his afflicted church, and to our everlasting comfort through our only mediator, redeemer, peacemaker, and lawgiver, Christ Jesus our Lord.

May the Holy Spirit rule our hearts in true fear of the Lord. So be it.

— *John Knox*

Teach us your mysteries

O Lord, the thoughts of my heart terrify me, and my heart trembles within me, because I sense that so many are born in vain.

What can I say, dear Lord? That you have ordained the wicked to wickedness? Far be it from me! I know, Lord, that you are eternally good, and that nothing wicked can be found in you. We are the works of your hand, created in Christ Jesus for good works. You have left many things to our choice. And you do not will the death of sinners, but you want them to repent and live.

You are the eternal light, and you hate all darkness. You desire that no one should perish, but that all should repent, come to the knowledge of your truth, and be happy.

O Lord God, you have loved us with an eternal love. You have chosen us before the foundation of the world, that we should be holy before you in love. You have done everything for us, for the best, in order that we should give honor to your name, and not to ourselves. What have we miserable sinners to boast about? What do we have that we have not received from you? All we have is from your fullness. For this, all who know your word thank you.

Dear Lord, the mystery of your holy word is not revealed to the rich, the honorable, or the wise, but to the poor, simple children. "Fear not, little flock, for it is your Father's good pleasure to give you the kingdom" (Luke 12:32).

So we miserable sinners pray that you would lead us in your truth and teach us your mysteries. Enable us to know the power of your covenant that you made with us in Christ, without any merit on our part—that you are ours, and we are yours. For your mystery will be found with those who fear you and those to whom you have made known your covenant. Amen.

— *Menno Simons*

Before I preach, a word of prayer

We give you our most heartfelt thanks, O most gracious and almighty God, that you have given us the ability to safely and without danger gather together in your name within this holy place.

Together we desire that you would inspire our hearts with the Holy Spirit, that I may utter your holy mysteries, and also that the believers here would faithfully receive those things which will be said.

And all this we pray to the glory of your name through our Lord Jesus Christ your most dear beloved son, amen.

— *Peter Martyr Vermigli*

Help us to learn our lessons well

Lord, you are the fountain of all wisdom and knowledge. As you allow me to learn, would you now also illuminate my understanding. Without you, I am blind. Strengthen my memory, if you will. And make my heart willing to receive—so this opportunity will not be canceled out by my ingratitude.

Grant me the power of your Spirit—the Spirit of all understanding, truth, judgment, wisdom, and learning. He will enable me to profit from these lessons, and the effort taken in teaching will not be in vain.

In whatever studies I undertake, Lord, help me to approach them with the right goals—to know you through our Lord Jesus Christ, to know fully the salvation of your grace, and to serve you uprightly according to your will.

Since you promise wisdom to the humble, and you confound the proud in the vanity of their wits, so make yourself known to those who have an upright heart. Make blind the ungodly and wicked. And I pray that you would fashion me in true humility, so I may be taught first to be obedient to you, then to those you have appointed over me.

I pray you would also fashion my heart to seek you without reservation, and to leave behind all evil and lusts of the flesh. That done, I may prepare to serve you in that place where you take me, when I am ready. Amen.

— *John Knox*

MAY YOUR WORD PENETRATE
OUR HEARTS

Blessed Lord, you have caused all holy Scriptures to be written for our learning. Grant now that we may hear, read, mark, learn, and inwardly digest these truths in such a way that, by the patience and comfort of your holy word, we may embrace and ever hold fast the blessed hope of everlasting life which you have given us in our Savior Jesus Christ.

May the words we have heard with our outward ears, through your grace, be grafted inwardly in our hearts. May they bring forth in us the fruit of good living, to the honor and praise of your name. Amen.

— *Thomas Cranmer*

LIGHT UP MY MIND

Father of mercies, wipe away all my iniquities through your Son and for his sake, crucified and raised up again for us.

Make me righteous with the righteousness of your only begotten son. Cleanse my heart with your Holy Spirit. Teach me your ways, and lead me in your truth.

And make clean my mind so that all wicked thoughts, corrupt affections, and dark ideas may depart far from me. Illuminate instead my thoughts with the light of your grace, so that I may crave only to do those things which please you—those things which are wholesome and profitable for the church of Christ. Amen.

— *Niels Hemmingsen*

We are going to study scripture—help us!

Almighty God, you have promised for your mercy's sake to govern us by your Holy Spirit, and to lead us into all truth. So first of all, we give you infinite thanks for so gracious and bountiful a promise. I have no doubt that you will keep it, and in the right way.

Further, because we are gathered together in your name, and the things we will discuss are important, then with all our heart we pray that you will give us your promised grace. Please moderate and direct that which we have taken upon ourselves—and so give glory to your name, truth to this place of study, and edification to your holy church.

We humbly ask of you: Please remove all our evil affections, and illuminate both our hearts and the hearts of those who hear us with the light of the holy Scriptures. Make plain all those things which seem to be obscure, and do not allow us to err in them.

And whatever matters that have not been rightly understood up to now (perhaps of many!), grant that they may now be more sincerely and faithfully perceived, through Jesus Christ our Lord, amen.

— *Peter Martyr Vermigli*

I seek you, Lord, before opening my Bible

Most merciful God and heavenly Father, in your great mercy you have caused the holy Scriptures to be written for our learning. But I am naturally blind. So grant me your good Spirit, by whose light my understanding will be illuminated to understand, and my memory confirmed and strengthened to retain what I read.

Then, by the blessing of the same Spirit, may your truth be so deeply rooted in my heart that everything I speak will bring forth fruits of blessing. And may it be always to the honor and glory of your holy name, the improvement and encouragement of those among whom I live, and to my own enduring peace and comfort, through Jesus Christ my only redeemer and advocate. So be it.

— John Downame

Before we study your word, a prayer

Almighty God, when we grapple with any of the central mysteries of our faith, we approach your goodness and mercy. All desire for argument is then laid away, our mind's turmoil is quieted, and we may sincerely seek out the truth.

Having found the truth, we may embrace it. And having obtained it, we may purely teach it.

So guide us in our discussion of your word by the direction of your Holy Spirit. As we study, and in those things about which we should be persuaded or dissuaded, we ask that we may not depart one iota from the sum of godliness. Rather, in whatever we imagine, think, and say, may it all be directed by your help and power—and to the honor of your name, through Christ our Lord, amen.

— Peter Martyr Vermigli

Grant me your wisdom

God of our fathers and Lord of mercy, you have made all things with your word. You have ordained in your wisdom that we should have dominion over the creatures you made, that we should order the world according to equity and righteousness, and that we should execute judgment with a true heart.

Give me wisdom and do not send me away from among your children. For I am your feeble servant, too young to understand your judgment and laws. And no matter how perfect a person may be, we are worth nothing without your wisdom.

Send your wisdom out of your holy heavens and from the throne of your majesty! May your wisdom be with me, and work with me, so I may know what is acceptable in your sight. Because wisdom knows and understands all things, wisdom will guide me in all that I do, and wisdom will preserve me in her power. So will my works be acceptable to you. Amen.

— *Primer of 1559*

IF YOU HEAR ME, YOU HEAR THE SON

O God our Father and Father of our Lord Jesus Christ,
I would not dare of my own initiative to be so bold as to
come before you to ask for anything—except that your
well-beloved Son has commanded me to do so.

Only in his name and at his command am I so bold.

So if you hear me, you hear your dearly beloved Son. And
if you do not hear me, then you do not hear Jesus Christ
himself, who has sent me to you, and has commanded me
to ask in his name.

This is the confidence that we have before him, that if we
ask anything according to his will he hears us (1 John 5:14).

Amen.

— *Thomas Cranmer*

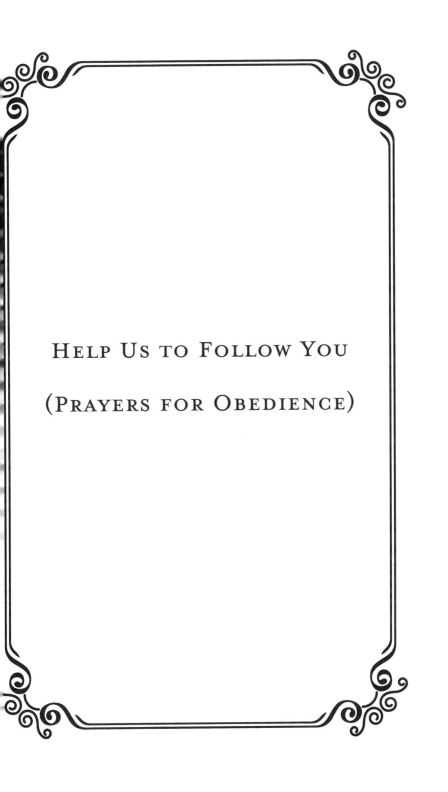

Help Us to Follow You

(Prayers for Obedience)

Give us a godly love

Good Lord, give us a godly love, so we may genuinely and with all our heart love you. You have so dearly loved us that you gave yourself as an offering.

Take away from us the love of worldly things. Though they appear so pleasant and beautiful, they are still just vanity—worthless, pointless, and futile. The world's fashions pass away. Make us abhor the filthy pleasures of the flesh, and keep us from being entangled in those pleasures. They lead only to shame and dishonor, corruption and destruction.

Kindle our hearts fervently with your love, so our only delight is you and your glory—and whatever matches your commands. May you be our only love, our delight, our joy, our happiness, our comfort. And whatever is without you or separated from your love, may we consider it more vain than vanity itself, more filthy than dung.

Grant also that out of our love for you, you would also grow in us a dynamic love toward our neighbors—even toward our enemies. Help us to love them from our heart even as we love ourselves. Help us to pray for them, help them, defend them, support them, provide for their needs, and treat them in all things as we wish to be treated.

Then I, being known by your badge, may be numbered with your disciples, and so through your mercy receive the reward of eternal glory.

O Lord God, you are love, and whoever lives in love lives in you, and you in them. Grant that in this world we may live together through love, you in us by your Holy Spirit, and we in you by faith. Then after we leave this world, we may find a home with you in your heavenly mansion, and so continue with you in glory forever and ever. Amen

— *Thomas Becon*

HELP US TO SEEK JUSTICE
IN OUR DAILY WORK

Dear Lord, help me to hate all underhanded deceit, and instead to love justice. Grant your comfort to the oppressed. Help those who do wrong to repent, and thieves and deceivers to make restitution.

Reveal yourself to those in positions of power—judges, landlords, the rich—that they might grow in love and compassion for the poor and the tenants.

And for laborers and artisans—give them strength to be diligent in their work. Amen.

— *John Bradford*

HELP US TO TRULY LOVE THOSE
WHO DO NOT LOVE US

O merciful God, grant us patience in adversity. Grant that sudden wrath would not overcome us, and that bitterness and desire for vengeance would not provoke to use uncharitable words that bring pain. Because when enemies fall upon us, speak against us, or bring up our faults, we think our retaliation would be justified.

No! Instead, help us to receive all adversity in love. May we may know as our best friends those who rebuke us most sharply.

Let no wicked root of envy, malice, or evil grow in us. No weariness or laziness. Give us strength to be willing and patient, with a fervent desire to suffer even more grievous things for your sake.

Pull up the wicked root of covetousness from us, and remove the vain shine of artificial spirituality. Save us from Satan's temptations.

Grant us love toward friends and enemies, that we may follow the nature of you our Father and the example of your only-begotten Son, Jesus Christ. Amen.

— *Myles Coverdale*

HELP US ALWAYS TO RESPECT
OUR NEIGHBOR

Merciful Father in heaven, give us your grace and help to love our neighbors from the heart, and to always do them good—both in words and deeds. Grant that we may live purely, avoiding offense to others, and provoking no one to unclean living. Help us to encourage others to honesty.

May we help others to save and keep what they have. And if they live in poverty, help us to relieve them as we are able.

May we never hurt others with a false witness, but instead always speak well of our neighbor.

Keep us from evil lusts and desires, never wanting what belongs to others.

For this is your will, and you have commanded us to be obedient.

Amen.

— Thomas Cranmer

Help us to walk as you did

Loving Lord, if we say we live in you, we ought to walk as you have walked. For you have called us to holiness. The blood of your Son Jesus Christ has cleansed us from all sin, not that we should continue in darkness, but rather walk in the light, as you are in the light.

"For we are his workmanship, created in Christ Jesus for good works, which God prepared beforehand, that we should walk in them" (Ephesians 2:10).

So take away our stony heart and give us a new, soft heart. Kill the old person in us, and fashion in us a new person, in your image, in right living and true holiness.

God of mercy, not everyone who says to you "Lord, Lord!" will enter your kingdom, but those who do the will of our Father in heaven. To confess you with our mouth but deny you with our deeds works to our condemnation—not our salvation. True knowledge of you consists not of talking, but in walking. Not in favoring, but in following. Not in loving, but in living.

To promise with our mouth that we will work in your vineyard, and yet work nothing at all ... that declares that we not really your children. So does bragging of justification by faith, and not bringing forth its fruits. Or glorying in the merits of Jesus Christ—in his blood, death, and suffering— but not living worthy of his kindness. Professing the gospel, but not walking according to its doctrine. Being baptized in your name, but not walking in new life...

What good is it all?

We are your friends if we do those things you commanded us to do.

We are your servants if we obey your will.

We are your sons and daughters if we honor and respect you according to your word.

We seek your glory if we attempt nothing that would dishonor you.

Grant then that our life may match what we profess, and that the light of our good works may so shine before others that they too may glorify you, our heavenly Father. Amen.

— Thomas Becon

LET US WORK WITHOUT A CARE

Dear and tender Father, our defender and nourisher, fill us with your grace. With it we may cast off the great blindness of our minds and our concern for worldly things, and instead concentrate on keeping your holy law.

With your grace we can work without worry for our everyday necessities, like the birds of the air and the lilies of the field. Without care—for you have promised to care for us. And you have commanded that we should cast all our care on you, as you live and reign, world without end, amen.

— Primer of 1559

Help me to truly follow you

Maker of heaven and earth, you have created a path for us to walk in, and you have commanded that we wander neither to the right nor to the left—according to your will, without adding our own good intentions or fleshly imaginations.

So as you have commanded, good Lord, give me the grace to do.

Help me not to follow my own will, nor the fancies of other people. And never let me be duped or beguiled by the mask of traditions, decrees, ancient laws, or any other person or thing that conflicts with your holy ordinances and commands.

Help me to faithfully believe and steadfastly confess that true godliness is only learned in your holy Bible. Then help me to order my life accordingly, to the praise of your holy name. Amen.

— *Thomas Becon*

Recover me and make me more like you

Almighty, everlasting God, I pray that you would draw me out of myself into you.

Grant that your love may recover again to me your grace.

Increase and make perfect in me that which is wanting. Raise up in me that which is fallen. Restore to me that which I have lost. Make alive in me that which is dead and should live.

And in all this may I conform to you in all my life and conversation—you dwelling in me and I in you, my heart supplied with your grace, and settled in your faith forever.

Lord, loose and set at liberty my spirit from all lesser things. Govern my soul, and work so that both in soul and body I may be holy and live to your glory, world without end, amen.

— *John Bradford*

Help us to know the same joy that we share

Lord, when we stand up to speak of the resurrection of Christ to others, give us grace so that we may be persuaded of it in our own hearts. May we find his gracious Spirit working in us, and as we speak of heaven and these joys to others, may we also find that joy in our own hearts. So that after this life is ended, we may reign with him in glory forever with Christ! To whom, with the Father, and the Holy Spirit, be all honor, praise, and glory forevermore. Amen.

— *Robert Rollock*

GIVE US THE RIGHT WORDS, AT THE RIGHT TIME

Lord, I appeal to you to finish the good work which you have begun. And if I ever build anything less worthily than I ought, cast it down. If I lay any other foundation than you yourself, destroy it. I ask so that your flock, led and inspired by your Spirit, may come to know that it will lack nothing—if led and fed by you as bishop and shepherd.

For you, O Son of God, are the defender and advocate of all who put their hope in you.

If you were to fail us, your name would be a weariness and mark of scorn to all. They would mock you as they mocked you hanging from the cross, for they would say: "He began to build and could not finish."

O then, sweet vine, whose vintner is the Father, and of whom we are the branches, do not abandon your planting and your building. You have promised to be near us to the fullness of the ages, and you have told us not to worry when brought before kings and rulers, for the Spirit would protect us at the critical moment, inspiring us with words so those rulers would even unwillingly hear testimony of you.

Would you put just the right words into the mouths of all who seek your glory? Purify your name, that we may speak before the princes of this world those things that are acceptable to you and profitable for all people.

For so it will happen that we, who are members one of another and one body in you—our one and everlasting head—will be your one and only bride, without spot or blemish (Ephesians 5:27).

You live and reign as God with the Father and the Holy Spirit, world without end. Amen.

— Huldrych Zwingli

KEEP THE SPOTLIGHT OFF US, LORD

Almighty God, since you have granted to us our place in life, help us to be content. And when you humble us, teach us to subject ourselves willingly to you, and to let you rule us. Keep us from wanting all the glory, which may lead us down the path to destruction.

Grant also that we may conduct ourselves so modestly in our various callings that you will always shine forth in us. Help us to focus on supporting and helping the believers to whom we are attached, in your sight—and so we will glorify your name among all people through Jesus Christ our Lord. Amen.

—John Calvin

WE ARE PILGRIMS—KEEP US ON THE ROAD

Help us to remember that we are pilgrims in the world, Lord. Let no splendor of wealth, power, or worldly wisdom blind our eyes, but may we always direct our eyes and all our senses toward the kingdom of your Son.

May we always fix our eyes there, and may nothing hinder us from hastening on in the course of our calling, until we finally reach the goal which you have set before us, and to which you invite us today by the proclaiming of your gospel.

Finally, would you gather us unto that happy eternity which has been obtained for us through the blood of your Son. May we never be separated from him. Sustained by his power, may we at last be raised by him to the highest heavens. Amen.

— John Calvin

YOU INVITE US TO STAY ON THE PATH

Father, we wander miserably in our thoughts. And in our attempts to worship you we only bring down the true and pure reverence of your divinity. We are easily drawn aside to warped superstition.

Grant that we may remain in pure obedience to your word, and never bend aside from it in any way. Teach us by the unconquered determination of your Spirit.

May we never yield to any terrors or threats of others, but persevere to revere your name, even to the end. However the world may rage after its own diabolic errors, may we never turn out of your path. May we continue in the right course—the one you have invited us to travel.

So, after finishing our race, we may arrive at that joy-filled rest which is laid up for us in heaven, through Christ our Lord. Amen.

— John Calvin

We are so timid, too timid

Almighty God, we are so fainthearted. None of us is prepared to follow where you may call us, but we may be motivated by the example of your servant Jonah to obey you in everything.

Though Satan and the world may oppose us with all their terrors, may we yet be strengthened by a reliance on the power and protection you have promised us. May we move ahead in the course of our vocation, our daily life, and never turn aside. And may we contend against all the hindrances of this world, until we reach that heavenly kingdom where we will enjoy you and Christ, your only begotten Son. He is our strength and salvation!

And may your Spirit bring us alive and strengthen all our natural abilities—so we may obey you, so we may glorify your name, and so we may finally share the glory to which you invite us through Christ our Lord. Amen.

— John Calvin

GIVE US COURAGE TO STAND

Almighty Lord God, you allowed Peter and all the apostles to have so great dread and cowardice in the time of your suffering. They all fled through fear of death—but afterwards, through the comfort of the Holy Spirit, you made them so strong that they were afraid of no man, nor of pain, nor of death.

Help us now by gifts of the same Holy Spirit. We are your poor servants, who all our lives have been cowards. Make us strong and bold in your cause, to maintain the gospel against those friends of hell who oppose you and against the tyrants of the world. Amen.

— John Wycliffe

BLESS YOUR WORD UNTO US

Lord, bless your word unto us, which now we have heard with our outward ears.

For those of us that you have reclaimed from any error in opinion or foolishness in life, make us also careful of passing along such errors or foolishness to others.

And for those of us still holding on to errors and foolishness, Lord, we pray that you would frame us according to your will, so that we may listen and follow your wisdom and turn our hearts to understanding.

Remove far from us all vain pretense of our own praises, and open our mouths to praise you, as often as needed for your glory.

Lord, wean us completely from any confidence in outward things, and instead settle all our confidence in yourself and your Son Christ Jesus. Amen.

— Henry Airay

Help me to speak of you—
from my heart

Lord, reform my heart, that your word may bear fruit in me.

May I hear your word with pleasure. And when I speak of you, and about the things of heaven, may the words come not from the teeth forward, but from the deepness of my heart, so that your word may edify both me and others.

If we are not duly prepared, Lord, it is a more dangerous thing to come to hear than to stay away. Better not to speak at all than to speak of heavenly things without the inward sense of the heart.

May you grant us grace, then, that in hearing and speaking of heavenly things, we may have this heavenly attitude in some measure, for Christ's sake. And to Christ, with the Father and Holy Spirit, be all praise, honor, and glory, both now and evermore. Amen.

— Robert Rollock

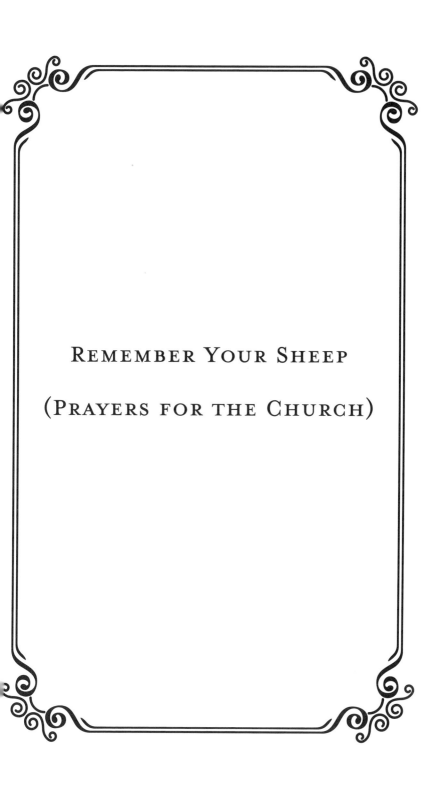

Remember Your Sheep

(Prayers for the Church)

LET ME PRAISE YOU FOREVER AND EVER

Lord, would you keep and rule our churches, our government, and our schools? Bestow a wholesome peace and leadership upon them.

And then gather and preserve an everlasting Christian church unto yourself in these lands. Purify and unite it by your Holy Spirit, that we may be one in you, in the true knowledge and worship of your dear Son, our Lord Jesus Christ, by and through him who for our sakes was nailed to the cross, and raised again from the dead.

Almighty, eternal son of God, faithful Lord and Savior Jesus Christ, you are the eternal word and image of the eternal Father, our mediator and savior. I give you my unbridled thanks for taking on our human nature, for being ordained as my redeemer, for suffering in the flesh and arising from the dead, and for interceding on my behalf.

I appeal to you now: Remember me and have mercy on me, for I am lonely and poor.

Increase the light of faith in me by your Holy Spirit. Bear with me in my weakness. Rule, protect, and purify me, for I have hoped in you, Lord. Let me never be put out and perplexed.

Almighty Holy Spirit: illuminate, rule, and sanctify me.

True, pure, and living Comforter: strengthen faith in my heart and soul.

Give me true hope and strength. Preserve and rule me, that I may dwell in the house of the Lord all the days of my life, that I may behold the beauty of the Lord, and that I may be and remain forever a holy temple of the Lord.

Let me praise you forever with a joyful spirit in that eternal heavenly church and congregation. Amen.

— *Philip Melanchthon*

WE REMEMBER OUR SPIRITUAL HERITAGE

Almighty God, you provided for your ancient church through the prophets, but you also designed a way for the fruit of their labors to continue to our age. Help us to remember and be thankful—and to take advantage of so great a benefit, so its fruit may grow for the glory of your name.

May we also learn to devote ourselves entirely to your service. And may each of us pay close attention to the work of our calling, so that we may strive together, with hearts united to promote the honor of your name—as well as the kingdom of your only-begotten Son—until we finish the battle and come at last to our heavenly rest, obtained for us by the blood of your only Son. Amen.

— *John Calvin*

KEEP US IN THE WAY OF TRUTH

We give you thanks, Almighty God and eternal Father of our Lord Jesus Christ, founder of your church. You are the wise, good, merciful, just, true, powerful sovereign.

Together with your coeternal Son and the Holy Spirit, you gather a heritage for your Son from among the human race, you maintain the ministry of the gospel, and you reformed the church through Martin Luther.

Now we offer our fervent prayer that you would from here on preserve, fix, and impress upon our hearts the doctrines of truth. By your Holy Spirit inflame our minds with a pure devotion. Direct our feet into the paths of holy obedience.

As we are committed to teaching others, we especially appeal to you to remember the perils that now threaten our entire world, from invasions to civil unrest. Our enemies corrupt the truth more boldly than ever. We pray that you may turn away these disasters. Help us to be more diligent in regulating our lives and directing our studies, always holding fast the idea that as long as we hang on to, listen to, learn, and love the pure teaching of the gospel, we will be in the house of God.

As the Son of God says, "If anyone loves me, he will keep my word, and my Father will love him, and we will come to him and make our home with him" (John 14:23).

Encouraged by this promise, I pray we will be quickened to teach the truth of heaven, remembering that the human race and governments are preserved for the sake of the church.

Help us fix our eyes on eternity. You have not revealed yourself and sent your Son in vain, but you truly love and care for those who magnify your benefits. Amen.

— *Philip Melanchthon*

I BELIEVE IN THE CHURCH

Lord, I believe and confess a holy universal Christian Church, which is the united communion of believers who confess one Lord, one God, one faith, and one baptism.

We are brought together, maintained, and ruled on earth by the only living and divine word, altogether beautiful and without blemish, unerring, pure, and blameless.

I confess publicly that you, my Lord Jesus Christ, by your blood have set apart the Church for yourself. You are her head and bridegroom, and you also will be with her to the end of the world.

Lord, grant that I and all those who believe in Christ may ultimately be found in this church. Grant that we would believe, teach, and hold all that you command us by your word. Root out all those things opposed that you have not planted. May we not be led into error by any human opinions, institutions, or doctrine of the old church leaders, universities, or old customs.

Amen.

— *Balthasar Hubmaier*

You will gather us!

We are humbled before you, most just and holy God. We with our sins do so much offend and provoke you to wrath and indignation. We confess your judgment to be just against us, and freely acknowledge all the sins and iniquities that in the word of God are presented against us.

We cry out and say along with the prophets that truly, Lord, you are righteous. You are true, and your judgments are just. But we are most unrighteous, liars, wicked. We are wholly overwhelmed with detestable iniquities. There is nothing sound or sincere within us. All what we have is corrupt and miserable.

We have sinned, we have been wicked, we have done unjustly, and we have forsaken you, Lord. We have rejected your servants the prophets, and we have not obeyed the words of your mouth.

Righteousness belongs to you, Lord.

So now as we lift up our minds to heaven, we give thanks to you, our Lord our God, who through your beloved Son has purged us and gathered us together to be a chosen people to yourself, and to be heirs of all your heavenly treasures.

May the Lord Jesus, the true and only shepherd of his church, bring home again lovingly the wandering sheep into his fold, and being gathered together in his church, preserve them forever.

To you therefore be all praise and glory, world without
end, amen.

— *Heinrich Bullinger*

A LAMENT FOR HOLY LIVING IN THE CHURCH

O, Savior, full of power and grace, can no prayers avail
with you? Will you not, for the honor of your name, and
for the sake of the light of your gospel, forgive these pitiful
people their multiplied transgressions against you?

Why does your anger still burn against your flock, as if
you intended to destroy everything, so that the future
appears even darker than the past?

We implore you, our blessed Lord, that you would form
out of all of us a pure and holy church, free from the worst
human traditions, so that Jesus and his commands will
alone be honored, in all purity and simplicity, so that we
may live in you without stain or blemish, and you in us,
by true faith, serving God our Father, who ever lives and
reigns with the Son and the Holy Ghost. Amen!

— *William Farel*

Help me to serve you in my work and beyond

O God, gracious Father, I thank you by your Son our dear Lord Jesus Christ, our only mediator and savior, for all your blessings and benefits, physical and spiritual, in time and eternity, which are many and greater than any creature can think or imagine.

Tender Father God, I pray you in your Son's name that you would preserve your Christian church around the world. Let your word be preached purely, cleanly, and rightly. And may your Son's kingdom be spread around the world, so that many would praise your mercy for all eternity.

O almighty God, protect your kingdom, rule all the leaders and states with your Holy Spirit, so that we may live peaceful lives, honoring God.

My dear Heavenly Father, forgive me my sin for your Son's death and pain's sake, and make me righteous with your Son's righteousness. Give me your Holy Spirit. Teach me your way. Lead me in your truth. Preserve my soul and protect me from ungodly thoughts, from results that poison, from harmful advice, from hardness of heart and rebellion, and from evil actions. Give me the mercy to think, to believe, and to do that which pleases you.

O Lord, give me understanding and help me to be diligent and faithful in my calling, for your honor and for the benefit of the Christian church and my neighbor. Preserve me in a living and quiet faith, in a good conscience until life's end. May I rest in the calling of my Lord Jesus Christ, and partake in his eternal life. And may I, with all your chosen ones, live, thank, and praise you forever.

We praise you and honor you together with your Son and the Holy Spirit, who are one God with you, now and forever, amen.

— *Niels Hemmingsen*

The way is so very narrow

O, Lord, Father, how very broad, easy, and pleasing to the flesh is the entrance into a miserable, carnal church.

But how wonderfully narrow, O Lord, is your way— the gate which leads into your poor and holy church (Matthew 7:13).

The way is so narrow that its gateposts strip off the gold and possessions, the flesh and blood, and all the lusts and inclinations of those who desire and sincerely seek to enter at this narrow gate.

And so, by your grace, we come to rest and remain forever in your holy church. Amen.

— *Menno Simons*

WE PRAY FOR CHURCH LEADERSHIP

Hear us, Lord. We appeal to you:

That we may abide in the unity of the church.

That we may remain in obedience to those set over us.

That you will teach the counterfeit leaders so much humility that they will regard themselves not as rulers set over us, but, according to Peter's words, as fellow elders (1 Peter 5:1).

That you will illumine them with your light, so they may know the true church which is your bride.

That you will open to them the fountain of living waters (Jeremiah 2:13).

That you will save us from the worn-out wells they have dug, containing no living water.

And that you will save us also from the unbearable burdens they lay upon our shoulders (Luke 11:46). Warn them to bear those burdens and practice what they preach.

If they cannot be persuaded in any other way to endure your easy yoke and light burden, force them to do it, O Lord!

Amen.

— *Huldrych Zwingli*

PURIFY YOUR CHURCH, LORD

Dear Father, in your mercy you have given me time to repent. Open then your law to me by your Holy Spirit, so I may know your will in it, love it, and always obey it.

Give me repentance.

May your Spirit sanctify me, and work in me a true taste of eternal life. Good, gracious Father, give me one little mouthful of the bread you fed to Elijah (1 Kings 19), so that I may also come to Horeb, your mountain.

Shelter your church, Lord, for Christ's sake. Purge your ministry from corruption and false ministers. Send out preachers to feed your people. Destroy the antichrist and all his kingdom. Help to repent those who have fallen, and keep others from falling.

Confirm the ministers and the poor in prison and exile; strengthen and deliver them in your truth. Strengthen them so they may answer their adversaries, and your servants will rejoice.

God of hosts, prove your own cause and help all your people—including me, as I need you most!

Amen.

— John Bradford

FOR ALL WHO WOULD BE PASTORS

Lord Jesus Christ, you are the true and everlasting Bishop, the mirror and pattern for all faithful pastors both in life and doctrine.

You came down from God your Father not only to be our Redeemer, but also our teacher, to open and declare to us the mysteries of the holy Scriptures.

We humbly pray now that in your mercy you would look upon your poor and scattered flock, whom you have purchased with your most precious blood. Send us shepherds who will diligently seek the lost sheep, lovingly carry them on their shoulders, and faithfully bring them home again.

Lord, you see how great the harvest is, and how few the workers. You are Lord of the harvest. Send us into the harvest!

And take away from us those false prophets who come to us in sheep's clothing, but inwardly are ravening wolves. Take away those false anointed and false preachers, who by their subtle doctrine would bring us into error.

Grant also, O Lord, that these true shepherds may accurately and reverently minister your holy mysteries to us: baptism and the Lord's supper. Through them may our faith be established, confirmed, and strengthened. And may we be comforted and made strong against the gates of hell, the devil, the world, the flesh, the curse of the law, sin, death, desperation, and all that is hostile to us.

May their shepherds' hands not be stretched out to receive, and slow to give. But establish in them a mind that is content, and willing to spend for the relief of the poor, that they may feed the flock both in word and deed.

You commanded your apostle Peter three times to feed your flock. And you gave this command not only to Peter, but to all your apostles—even to all pastors who follow.

Deal with your flock, most faithful Shepherd, according to your promise. Raise up faithful and diligent shepherds who may feed their flocks with your life-filled word, lead a good life, and maintain hospitality for the comfort of the poor. And in all things may they behave according to your will and commandments. So when you, the most high Bishop and chief Shepherd, appear, may they receive the pure and spotless crown of glory. Amen.

— *Thomas Becon*

Grant us unity in the battle

O God, grant us true love and unity. Take from us all division and lack of harmony. Gather us together through your Holy Spirit. Remove all discord and disunity from your holy church.

Give us patience in adversity. Send your godly comfort and joy unto all who are in distress and trouble for your name's sake.

Strengthen the weak, lift up the feeble, and establish the doubtful. And in the battle help those who are yours—so that in you they may overcome all danger and harm. Amen.

— *Myles Coverdale*

Help your church through this storm

Lord Jesus Christ, through your almighty power you made us all. You govern all. And by your unspeakable goodness you bring everything to life.

Turn your gaze now to your beloved, your church. You see the storms that toss your little ship about. We will all drown if we sink!

We confess that our own sins have caused this storm, but we have endured so much. We are worn out by wars, troubled by plagues and floods, scared by strange threats. Yet it seems there is nowhere to rest, and worse to come. We appeal to your mercy, not for any worthiness of ours, but for your glory.

When you slept on the boat and the storm threatened, you awoke from the cry of just a few disciples. At your voice, the wind and waves grew still. Now, in this far more serious storm, many souls are in danger. We beg you to awake at the cry of your church. Many thousands now cry out: "Lord save us, or we perish!"

This storm surpasses all our best efforts. In fact, our best efforts only make things worse. We need your voice, Lord Jesus. Just say "Storm, be still," and things will grow calm.

You would have spared thousands in Sodom and Gomorrah, if there were just ten righteous. Now there are many thousands who love the glory of your name. At their pleading, will you not remember your mercy?

Demons fled your voice when you walked this earth.
Lord, now drive away the schoolmasters of riot, coveting,
ambition, sexual sin, vengeance, and discord. "Create in
me a clean heart, O God, and renew a right spirit within
me. Cast me not away from your presences, and take not
your Holy Spirit from me. Restore to me the joy of your
salvation" (Psalm 51:10–12).

By this Spirit you have assembled and knit so many
tongues, nations, and different people into the one body
of your church. We cling to you by the same Spirit. So if it
may please you to renew the Spirit in all our hearts, these
outward calamities will cease. Or if they do not, they will
at least turn to the advantage of those who love you.

Set confusion in order, O Lord, and let your Spirit spread
forth upon waters of wavering opinions. Grant that, as all
who dwell in your house have but one law, one baptism,
one God, one hope, and one Spirit, so also there may be
but one voice among all those who profess your truth.

Give to your struggling church today what you gave her at
her start. Give us leaders who are in awe of you. Give your
shepherds the gift of prophecy, that they may interpret the
scriptures not by human reason, but by your inspiration.
Give them the threefold love which demanded of Peter
when you told him to feed your flock. Give your people a
willingness to obey your ways.

You spared the Ninevites as soon as they repented. Will
you turn away from your spouse, casting herself at your feet
with sighs instead of sackcloth, and tears instead of ashes?

You have promised forgiveness to such a convert. You are the Maker, the Ransomer, the Savior. Repair your creation! Do not allow us to perish! We depend wholly on you.

Be present in us, so your church may with one mind and voice give thanks to the Father, Son, and Holy Spirit—the perfect pattern of harmony, distinct and yet in nature but one, to whom be praise and glory forever. Amen.

— Book of Christian Prayers of 1578

LET YOUR SHEPHERDS BE CLOTHED WITH RIGHTEOUSNESS

O Lord, let your shepherds be clothed with righteousness, and let your saints rejoice.

Pour out your Spirit of wisdom on these ministers of your word, so they may know the mysteries of your holy will. Give them the gift of utterance, that they may set forth the abundant riches of your gospel. Write your laws in their hearts, and your testimonies in their innermost parts, that they may lead your people into all truth, and guide your church with discretion.

Make them good workers, faithful shepherds, and wise builders. Help them to mend any broken walls and feed your sheep with the bread and water of life. Strengthen them to care for your vineyard, repair your sanctuary, and lift up those who are dedicated to the service of the Lord.

Finally, may they shine with such a holy and pure light before us that they may edify no less by example of life than by instruction of teaching. So as we see the qualities you have given them to benefit the church—their modesty, meekness, endurance, patience, and more—may many others also be won to your gospel through their holiness, to confess the glory of your name. And we will see that you surely live, reign, and work in your servant. Amen.

— Book of Christian Prayers of 1578

Protect and defend your church, Lord!

Almighty God, you see how your Church today is miserably torn by many conflicts. You see how there are so many traitorous ministers who continue to plague it.

Help us to experience what you have promised in Scripture by your prophet: That you will be the perpetual guardian of your chosen people—people you have received and embraced so they can move ahead with courage through any conflict and emerge as conquerors.

Would you also now stretch out your hand against the sin you have denounced? Reduce to nothing not only those who oppose you and your servants and your children, but also those serpents who harass and torment your church through intrigue, fraud, and other indecent means.

Do this until at last we see a full triumph in your kingdom, together with Christ Jesus, our Lord and head. Amen.

— John Calvin

PROTECT YOUR CHURCH AND KEEP US FROM FALLING

Holy, righteous, and wise one. Mighty, terrible, and fearful Lord God. Judge of all and governor of all the world. Patient and gracious Father, whose eyes are upon our ways…

Wash us from our wickedness and pour out your Holy Spirit upon us. Take from us our hard hearts, our stony hearts, our unrepentant hearts, our distrusting and doubtful hearts. Take our carnal, our secure, our idle and foolish hearts. Take away our impure, arrogant, envious, impatient, covetous hearts.

Give us new hearts instead: soft hearts, faithful hearts, merciful hearts. Obedient, pure, holy hearts. True, simple, lowly, and penitent hearts. Give us hearts to fear and trust you forever. Write your law in our hearts, graft it in our minds.

Grant us a spirit of prayer and make us diligent and happy in what you give us to do. Take our souls and bodies into custody forever. Take our lives and all that we have, and give us whatever you know we need. Guide us always as your children, so our lives and our deaths will praise you through Jesus Christ.

We pray for ourselves, but also for others—those in exile or in prison, in misery or heaviness, in poverty or sickness.

If it is your will, send your holy word and faith among us in this place and this country once again. Turn the hearts of those who speak against us. Have mercy on our families and fellow believers, our neighbors and those whose lives you have linked to ours.

And for those here gathered in your holy name, grant your blessing and Holy Spirit to dwell in us and set us apart. Keep us as your children, today and forever. Keep us from all evil for your glory, our good, and for the good of the church. Strengthen those who stand, so they do not fall. Lift up those who have fallen, and keep us from falling, through Jesus Christ, our Lord and only Savior, who lives and reigns with you in the Holy Spirit, and to whom be all praise and honor, now and forever, amen.

— John Bradford

PRESERVE THE CHURCH AND GIVE US PEACE

Most merciful heavenly Father, I pray in the name of your only begotten Son: defend your church and congregation in all parts of the world!

Confirm the purity of your word, that the kingdom of your Son may increase throughout all the world, and that many may declare your goodness and mercy forever.

Give also unto this land a safe and peaceable governance, under your protection. Govern with the Holy Spirit and sovereign, with the leaders of the realm, that we may lead a quiet life in all godliness and honesty, to your glory. Amen.

— Niels Hemmingsen

You alone are the hope of the world

I place my hope in your mercy, Lord, from everlasting to everlasting. Do not let me be disappointed.

Sovereign Lord, have mercy on us, and be reconciled to us. Grant us peace, Lord. You are the hope of all the earth.

Please crown the year with your goodness. Open your hand and fill all living things with your plenty, and prosper the work of our hands.

Remember your church around the globe, for you have established it and redeemed us with your blood. We lift up those who bear fruit for you, who remember the poor and needy. For earthly things grant them heavenly gifts. For corruptible, incorruptible. For temporary, eternal.

We also lift up to you those Christians who are persecuted and who need you, also our brothers and sisters in captivity. Grant return to those who wander, health to the sick, and deliverance to the captives.

We lift up our government and its leaders, all power and authority, as well as our church leadership. And here in the church, preserve our marriages, nourish our infants, guide our youth, sustain our aged, comfort the weak-hearted, gather together the scattered, bring back the wanderers, and knit us together in your church body.

Set free those who are troubled, voyage with the voyagers, travel with the travelers, stand up for the widows, shield the orphans, rescue the captives, heal the sick. Whatever trouble or difficulty we face, remember us, O God.

Remember all who love us, and those who dislike us. And those we have not mentioned, Lord, remember them too. You know what each one needs.

For you, O Lord, are the help of the helpless, the hope of the hopeless, the savior of the storm-tossed, the harbor of the voyager, the physician of the sick. You are all things to all people.

You know each request, each home and their needs. Deliver this community, Lord, and the country where we sojourn. Keep us from pandemic and hunger, earthquake and flood, fire and invasion and war.

End the divisions in our churches, still the ragings of those who do not know you, and receive us into your kingdom as children of light. Grant us your peace and love.

And at the close of our life, Lord, direct us in peace. Gather us together under the feet of your elect, whenever and however you choose, only without shame and sins.

Lord, be within me to strengthen me, without me to guard me, above me to shelter me, beneath me to uphold me, before me to direct me, after me to bring me back, and round about me to secure me.

Amen.

— Lancelot Andrewes

As we worship together, we pray

Lord, you hear the prayers of all who come before you. I come, too. In spite of our sins, Lord, have mercy.

You will open my lips, and my mouth will speak your praises. I will come into your house, riding on your mercy. In fear of you I will worship.

We wait for your loving kindness, O God, in the midst your temple. Remember, O Lord, all the believers who surround me in prayer, even now. Remember them for the sake of their sincere passion. And in your mercy please also remember those who, for good reasons, could not be here with us today.

Lord, I have loved this gathering place, where your honor dwells—where we hear the voice of thanksgiving, and the story of your wondrous works.

"One thing have I asked from the LORD, that I will seek after: that I may dwell in the house of the LORD all the days of my life, to gaze upon the beauty of the LORD and to inquire in his temple" (Psalm 27:4).

"You have said, 'Seek my face.' My heart says to you, 'Your face, LORD, do I seek'" (Psalm 27:8).

"Open to me the gates of righteousness, that I may enter through them and give thanks to the LORD" (Psalm 118:19).

"That your eyes be open night and day toward this house, the place of which you have said, 'My name shall be there,' so that you may listen to the prayer that your servant offers toward this place" (1 Kings 8:29).

Amen.

— *Lancelot Andrewes*

Defend your church, Lord

Lord Jesus, it is your holy gospel. It is your cause. Remember all the many troubled hearts and consciences, your churches and your little flocks, which suffer terror and distress from the devil.

Preserve and establish your truth!

Bring to nothing all hypocrisy and lies, and give peace and unity, so that your honor may advance and your kingdom may flourish and increase without ceasing against the gates of hell.

O Son of God and Immanuel, who was crucified for us and did rise again! We appeal to you: Rule, defend, and preserve your church. Amen.

— *Philip Melanchthon*

Guide, govern, and prosper us

O Lord God, who are we that you should show us such
great mercy?
Most loving Lord, forgive for Christ's sake our
unthankfulness and all our sins.

Increase the Holy Spirit in us to teach our hearts to cry
"Abba, Father!" and to assure us of our eternal election in
Christ, to live joyfully in your will more and more, and to
confirm us in your truth—that we may live and die in it.

By the power of the same Spirit, may we boldly give
an account of our faith to all—but with humility and
meekness. So even if others slander us as evildoers, they
may be ashamed and quieted when they see our good way
of life in Christ Jesus.

We ask you for his sake, Lord God, to guide, govern, and
prosper us as we gather as believers to praise your holy
name. And we pray you would not only be present here
with your children according to your promise, but also
that you would help the persecuted believers gathered
in other places. May they and we, consenting together in
one Spirit and truth, seek your honor and glory in all our
assemblies. So be it.

—*John Knox*

Teach Us to Pray and Share

(The Lord's Prayer and Communion)

MAY I NOT COVET—NOT EVEN THEIR DOG

Father, I know that I should not wish for my neighbor's (nicer) house, or my neighbor's (more beautiful/handsome) spouse. I must not think to myself that I should have anything belonging to someone else—not even the smallest thing. Not even their dog.

In the other nine commandments you have forbidden all injuries and evil practice against my neighbors. Now you charge me to beware of thinking any evil thought against them.

And for that reason I have great reason to praise you: You care about my home and everything I own (even my dog) that you command everyone else never to wish they had all my things, instead of me.

The apostle said we should be "casting all your anxieties on him, because he cares for you" (1 Peter 5:7). It is true, and I find it true. In this way you care for us, and so you would have us care for one another.

But, gracious Lord, I must confess that I have forgotten and broken this commandment, and I still do every day. I am wishing and woulding every minute of every hour. I could have been content, but I have always thought my neighbor had too much, and I too little. And the dregs of these things, Lord, are not quite out of my heart. I deserve your severe justice.

But keep in mind the frailty of my flesh, the corruption of my nature, and the many temptations. Remember how I am able to do nothing of myself—and how I would come to nothing if left to myself. Be merciful to me and pardon me in this way also, for the sake of your son. Amen.

— John Bradford

WRITE YOUR LAWS ON MY HEART

Set my heart straight, Lord. May I worship no other God. May I reverence your name. And may I remember your Sabbath rest.

Set my heart right in all that I say. Help me to honor my parents, to obey rulers, and reverence the ministry of the gospel.

Keep my hands clean from blood and true from theft. Keep my body free from adultery and my tongue devoid of all offense.

But purge my heart first, Lord—and then my hands, eyes, tongue, and feet. Then my whole body will be that much cleaner.

Write all these laws on my heart, O Lord, and on the hearts of all your faithful people. May we believe your ways and keep them all the days of our lives, to your glory and praise, through Jesus Christ our Savior. Amen.

— John Bradford

Teach us to keep your name holy

Almighty God, dear heavenly Father, your holy name
has been so cheapened and debased in this wretched
valley of sorrow. It has been blasphemed, put to shame,
dishonored, abused, and made a cloak for sin. So grant us
your divine grace, that we may be on our guard against
everything which does not serve to praise and honor your
holy name.

We pray that all witchcraft and sorcery may be done away.
That all conjuring of the devil or of creatures by your
name may cease. That all false beliefs and superstitions
may be rooted out. That all heresy and false doctrine
which disguise themselves with your name may come to
nothing. That no false pretense of truth, piety, or holiness
may deceive anyone. And that none may swear, lie, or
deceive by your name.

Protect us against all false confidence pretending to rest
upon your name. Protect us against all spiritual pride and
the pompous ego of worldly honor or reputation.

Dear Father, may your name be made holy in us. For
I confess that I have (to my shame!) often dishonored
your name. And I do so still. Through pride and through
seeking my own honor and the glory of my name, I
blaspheme yours. Therefore help me by your grace. May
my name cease to be anything to me. May I recognize my
nothingness, so that you alone and your name and honor
may be in me.

Help us in all our necessities and weaknesses to call upon your holy name. Help us in anguish of conscience and in the hour of death not to forget your name. Help us with all our goods and in all our words and works to praise and honor you alone, and never to seek a name for ourselves— but only for you, whose alone are all things.

Preserve us from the shameful vice of ingratitude. Grant that by our good works and life all others may be stirred to praise, not us, but you in us, and to honor your name. Help us, that our evil works or weaknesses may give no one a reason to stumble and dishonor your name or to cease from praising you.

Keep us, that we may not desire any worldly or eternal blessing which is not to the honor and praise of your name. And if we pray for such things, do not listen to our folly. Help us so to live that we may be found true children of God, that your Father-name may not be named upon us falsely or in vain.

We offer this petition with every psalm and prayer in which we praise, honor, thank, and sing to you—and here belong all our hallelujahs, amen.

— Martin Luther

MAY YOUR KINGDOM COME IN OUR LIVES

Lord, life on this world is a kingdom of sin and wickedness, under one lord, the evil spirit. But your kingdom is a kingdom of every grace and virtue under one Lord, Jesus Christ your dear Son—the source of every grace and virtue.

So help us, dear Father, and be gracious to us. Above all things, grant us a true and constant faith in Christ, a fearless hope in your mercy despite all the fearfulness of our sinful conscience, and a thorough love for you and those around us. Keep us from unbelief, despair, or revenge.

Guard us also against indecency and give us a love for innocence and all purity. Steer us away from division, war, and discord, and let the virtue of your kingdom come—in peace, unity, and quiet rest.

Grant that neither wrath nor any other bitterness may set up its kingdom within us. Instead, by your grace, may sweet simplicity and neighborly devotion rule within us, along with all kindliness, love, and gentleness. Help us to experience no undue sorrow or sadness, but let joy and gladness in your grace and mercy come to us.

And help us, finally, that all sin may be turned away from us, so that we may be filled instead with your grace, along with all virtue and good works, and thus become your kingdom. With all our heart, mind, and spirit, and with all our powers of body and soul, may we obediently serve you, keep your commandments, and do your will. May we be ruled by you alone, and not follow after self or flesh, devil or world.

Grant that your kingdom, now begun in us, may increase and daily grow in power. May indifference to serving you—that subtle wickedness—never overcome us or make us fall away. Instead, give us the power and earnest purpose not only to make a beginning in righteousness, but to boldly go on unto completeness. As David says, "light up my eyes, lest I sleep the sleep of death, lest my enemy say, 'I have prevailed over him'" (Psalm 13:3–4).

Help us to remain constant, so your future kingdom may be completed. Help us to long for the life to come and to not fear death. Take away from us the love of living here, and all dependence on this present life, that your kingdom may in us be made perfect and complete. Amen.

— Martin Luther

WE REMEMBER YOUR MERCY (BEFORE COMMUNION)

God our Father, for the tender mercy and merits of your Son, be merciful to us. Forgive us all our sins, and give us your Holy Spirit to purge, cleanse, and sanctify us.

Make us holy in your sight through Christ—ready and worthy to receive this holy communion with its fruits, to rejoice and fully strengthen our hearts in the Lord.

To you be all honor and glory, and all praise forever, world without end. Amen.

— John Bradford

Your will be done

Your will is always best, dear Father, loved above all things and most to be desired. So be merciful to us and let nothing be done according to our own will.

Teach us and allow us to have real and perfect patience when our will is broken or hindered. If anyone says or does anything contrary to our will, help us not to be angry or wrathful, and not complain, curse, cry out, judge, condemn, or accuse. Instead, help us in all humility to let our own will go and to give place to those who hinder or even oppose us. Help us to praise, bless, and do good to those who, against our own will, fulfill your divine will— which is altogether good.

Give us grace to willingly bear illness, poverty, shame, suffering, and adversity, and to know that these are your divine will for the crucifying of our will. Help us to bear even injustice gladly, and hold us back from taking revenge, from returning evil for evil, or resisting force with force. Instead, grant us grace to take pleasure in your will, which lays these things upon us, and to give you praise and thanks.

Do not let us simply blame the devil or wicked people for anything contrary to our will, but help us to credit only your divine purpose, which orders all such things to keep our will in check and increase our blessings in your kingdom.

Help us to die willingly and joyfully, and to welcome death as a manifestation of your will, so that impatience and despair may not make us disobedient toward you. Help us so that all our members—eyes, tongue, heart, hands, feet—be not submissive to their own desires or will, but be taken captive, imprisoned and broken in your will. Preserve us from all evil, and from that rebellious, obstinate, stubborn, and fickle self-will.

Grant us a true obedience—a submissiveness that is simple and complete in all things, from the spiritual to the worldly, earthbound to eternal. Preserve us from the cruel vice of false accusations, slander, back-biting, malicious judging, condemning, and accusing of others. Keep far from us the great unhappiness and grievous plague of tongues like these. Instead, teach us to hold our peace when we see or hear in others things that seem blameworthy and (to us) displeasing. Help us to cover them over, to complain to no one but you, to give them over to your will, and thus heartily forgive our debtors and have sympathy with them.

Teach us to know that no one can do us any harm, except by first doing themselves a thousandfold greater harm in your eyes. With that in mind, may we be moved to mercy rather than anger, and to pity rather than revenge.

In the end, help us not to rejoice when it goes poorly for those who have not done our will or have hurt or displeased us. Help us also not to be disturbed when it goes well for them. Amen.

— Martin Luther

Give us our true daily bread

The daily bread is our Lord Jesus Christ, who feeds and comforts the soul. So would you grant us grace, Heavenly Father, to make known and preserve Christ's life, words, works, and sufferings to all the world?

May his words and works remain before us all our life as a powerful example and mirror of all that is good and right. Help us during times of suffering or misfortune to find strength and comfort in and through his cross and his suffering. Help us in firm faith to overcome our own death by his death, and so boldly to follow our beloved leader into the other life.

Grant your grace to all preachers, that they may proclaim Christ and your word, for salvation and for the benefit of all, throughout the world. Help all who hear the preaching of your Word to learn Christ, and so honestly to live better lives.

Graciously drive out of your church all strange preaching and teaching from which we do not learn Christ. Grant that all hurtful, heretical, erroneous, and merely human doctrines may cease, and your word alone, which is our true bread of life, may be distributed. Have mercy on all clergy and all that are in church authority, that they may be enlightened by your grace to teach and govern us rightly by what they say and how they live their lives.

Preserve all who are weak in faith, that they may not stumble at the wicked example of their rulers.

Preserve us from any heretical or apostate teachers, that we may remain one, and partake of one daily bread—the daily doctrine and word of Christ.

Graciously teach us to regard rightly the sufferings of Christ, receive them into our hearts, and form them in our lives, to our salvation.

And would you "Give us our daily bread," that is, may Christ abide in us and we in him forever, and may we worthily bear his name, the name of *Christian.* Amen.

— Martin Luther

Lend us your grace (after communion)

Lord Jesus Christ, our redeemer, we give you forever honor and praise for feeding our souls with this spiritual and heavenly food.

We look to you for your tender mercy. You have given this communion celebration to us as an observance of ongoing thankfulness, of daily remembrance, and of loving unity.

Even so, merciful Savior, please lend us your grace. May we be thankful to you not only for our redemption, purchased through your death and shed blood, but also that in this observance we would increase in love toward you, and toward all others for your sake.

— Myles Coverdale

Forgive us our debts, and remove our heavy burdens

O Father, comfort our conscience now and in our last hour, otherwise it is now and will be in grievous terror because of our sin and your judgment.

So send your peace into our hearts, that we may await your judgment with joy. Do not enter with us into the sharpness of your judgment, for then no one will be found righteous.

Teach us, dear Father, not to rely on or comfort ourselves with our own good works or merits. Instead, we boldly cast ourselves upon your boundless mercy alone.
In the same way, do not let us despair because of our sinful life. We are so obviously guilty. Instead, we regard your mercy higher and broader and stronger than all our life.

Help all those who feel the anguish of despair in the hour of temptation or death. Comfort them and receive them into grace. Forgive them and all of us our sins. Trade your good for our evil, as you have commanded us to do to others.

Silence also the evil spirit—the cruel slanderer, accuser, and magnifier of our sins—now, at our last hour, and in all anguish of conscience, even as we too refrain from slander and from magnifying the sins of others.

Do not judge us according to the accusation of the devil or our miserable conscience. And do not listen to the voice of any enemies who may accuse us, even as we too do not listen to those who accuse and slander others.

Remove from us the heavy burden of sin and conscience, so that with light and joyous hearts we may live and die, do and suffer ... trusting wholly in your mercy. Amen.

— Martin Luther

GIVE US OUR DAILY BREAD—
BUT NOTHING MORE

Lord, give us all that the necessity of this life requires, day by day. We do not want to store up a supply that would last for many years, to preclude all necessity of praying to you. We do not want to forget you.

But minister it day by day, so that we may daily feel your benefits and never forget you.

Or if you give us an abundance above what we desire, then give us a heart to use it for the purpose you intend— including sharing with our neighbors. Help us not to be overly attached to what you provide, but to remember it is yours, and that you may take it away whenever you like.

In that way help us to be content with whatever you do, always keeping in mind that whatever you provide is simply our daily bread.

Amen.

— William Tyndale

Lead us not into temptations—
all of them

Dear Father, grant us grace to control the lust of the flesh. Help us to resist the desire to eat, drink, or sleep too much, or to be idle and lazy. Help us by fasting, and by moderation in food, dress, sleep, and work, by staying alert and working, so that we may bring the flesh into subjection and fit it for good works.

Help us to fasten the evil, impure tendencies or desires of the flesh with Christ upon the cross, and to slay them, so that we may not give in to any of their temptations. When we see a beautiful person or image or any other creature, help us not to see it as a temptation, but as an opportunity to love purity and to praise you for your creation. And when we hear sweet sounds or feel things that please the senses, help us not to seek lust, but rather your honor and praise.

Preserve us from the great vice of greed and the desire for this world's riches. Keep us, that we may not seek the world's honor and power, nor give in to the desire for them. Preserve us from walking in the path of the world's deceit, pretense, and false promises. Preserve us, so the world's wickedness and tragedy may not lead us to impatience, revenge, wrath, or other vices. Help us to renounce the world's lies and deceits, its promises and unfaithfulness, and all its good and evil. Instead, help us to abide firmly in this renunciation and to grow in it from day to day.

Preserve us from the suggestions of the devil, that we may not give in to pride, become self-satisfied, and despise others for the sake of riches, rank, power, knowledge, beauty or other good gifts of yours. Preserve us from falling into hatred or envy for any cause. Preserve us from yielding to despair, that great temptation of our faith—not now, and not at our last hour.

Heavenly Father, keep all who strive and work against these great temptations. Strengthen those who still stand, and raise up those who have fallen or are overcome. And grant your grace to us all, that in this desperate and uncertain life, where we are constantly surrounded by so many enemies, we may fight with endurance, with a firm and noble faith, and win the everlasting crown. Amen.

— *Martin Luther*

YOU HAVE NOURISHED AND FED OUR SOULS (AFTER COMMUNION)

Almighty God, most merciful Father, you open your gracious hand, whereby all living things have their food in due season.

We give you honor, praise, and thanks for all your benefits, spiritual and physical, which you have richly poured upon us. We deserve none of it. But we especially thank you for this worthy memorial of our redemption, in which you have nourished and fed our souls with the body and blood of your dear Son, our Savior Jesus Christ, who is blessed for ever.

— *Myles Coverdale*

Deliver us from evil, amen

Deliver us, O Father, from your eternal wrath and from the pains of hell. Deliver us from your strict judgment, in death and at the last day. Deliver us from sudden death. Preserve us from water and fire, from lightning and hail. Preserve us from famine and scarcity. Preserve us from war and bloodshed. Preserve us from your great plagues, pandemics, and other grievous diseases.

Preserve us from all evils and physical necessities, yet in such a way that in all these things your name may be honored, your kingdom increased, and your divine will be done.

God help us, without doubting, to obtain all these petitions, and let us never doubt that you have heard us and will hear us in them all—and that it is "Yes," not "No," and not "Perhaps."

The things which I have prayed for, I do not doubt. They are certainly right and will be granted, not because I have prayed for them, but because you have commanded us to pray for them, and have surely promised to give them. I am certain that you, God, are true and cannot lie. Therefore, not the worthiness of my prayer, but the certainty of your truth makes me firmly believe, with every doubt removed, that it will become an amen and be an amen.

So we say with joy, "Amen. It is true and certain." Amen.

— *Martin Luther*

A PRAYER TOGETHER AS WE SHARE COMMUNION

O Lord, we acknowledge that no creature is able to comprehend the length or breadth, the depth or the height of your most excellent love—which moved you to show mercy where none was deserved.

You gave life where death had gotten the victory. You recovered us into your grace plan when we did nothing but rebel against your justice.

Lord, the blind dullness of our corrupt nature does not allow us to experience your ample benefits. Even so, at the command of our Lord Jesus Christ, we present ourselves to this table—which he left us to be used in remembrance of his death, until he comes again.

Here we declare and witness before the world that by him alone we have received liberty and life. By him alone you acknowledge us as your children and heirs. By him alone we have access to the throne of your grace. By him alone we are members of this spiritual kingdom, to eat and drink at his table. By him alone we have a place in heaven. And by him alone our bodies will be raised up from the dust, and join him in that endless joy which you have prepared for your elect before the foundation of the world was laid.

All these blessings are beyond our comprehension. We acknowledge and confess that we have received them only by your free mercy and grace, by the only beloved Son Jesus Christ. And as your congregation, moved by the Holy Spirit, we give you all thanks, praise, and glory, forever and ever. Amen.

—*John Knox*

The Lord's Prayer, expanded

Our Father in heaven, we your children here on earth
ask that you will look on us in your mercy. Lend us your
grace, that we may lift up your name among us and in
all the world—though a pure and sincere teaching of the
word, through earnest compassion in our daily living, and
through everything that we say.

In your grace, separate us from all false doctrine and evil
living that would blaspheme and slander your holy name.

Let your kingdom come, and let it be great. Bring all sinful,
blind people—captives of the devil in his kingdom—to the
knowledge of true faith in Jesus Christ your Son.

Strengthen us, Lord, with your Spirit, to do and to
experience your will both in life and death, in prosperity
and need. May our own will always be broken, offered up,
and mortified.

And give us our daily bread. Preserve us from covetous
desire, and from worrying what we should eat, so that we
may be assured to have abundance of all good things—
from you.

Forgive us our trespass, as we forgive those who offend us.
Then our heart will have a sure and glad conscience and
never fear, nor be afraid of any sin.

Lead us not into temptation, but help us through your
Spirit to subdue the flesh, to disregard the world with its
vanities, and to overcome the devil with his crafty assaults.

And finally, deliver us from all evil, both physical and spiritual, here in time and eternal. Amen.

— *Myles Coverdale*

INCREASE THE FERVOR OF OUR LOVE (AFTER COMMUNION)

Lord God Almighty, with all our hearts we thank you for feeding our souls with the body and blood of your most dear Son.

And we beg you genuinely to illuminate our minds with your Holy Spirit. Increase the strength of our faith daily. Increase our assurance of hope in your promises. And increase the fervor of our love toward you and our neighbors, to the glory and praise of your holy name. Amen.

— *Myles Coverdale*

"Our Father," not "my Father"

Almighty God, we have sinned so often and so grievously against your divine and gracious will. We have surely angered you. Yet in your boundless mercy you have granted us permission to look to you and call you *Father*. In fact, through the merit and mediation of your only beloved Son, our Lord Jesus Christ, you have actually taught and *commanded* us to do so—though you might justifiably judge us sternly as sinners.

Now in your mercy, place in our hearts a comfortable confidence in your fatherly love. Make us taste and feel the sweetness of childlike trust, so that we may with joy call you Father. So that we may know and love you. So that we may call upon you for everything we need.

Hold us in your keeping, dear Father, that we may remain your children, and never be guilty of making you into a terrible judge—and we your enemies.

It is your will that we not only call you Father, but that all of us *together* call you our Father. In that way we will offer our prayers with one accord for all. Grant us then brotherly love and unity, that we may know and think of one another as true brothers and sisters, and that we would pray to you as our one common Father, for all and everyone, even as one child prays for another to its father.

Let no one among us seek our own interests or forget before you the interests of others. Instead, as we lay aside all hatred, envy, and division, may we love one another as good and true children of God, and so say with one accord not "my Father," but "our Father."

You are not a father according to the flesh nor upon earth, but you are in heaven—a spiritual Father. You never die and you are not weak. You are not like an earthly father who cannot help himself. You have shown us how immeasurably better a Father you are. Compared to you, all earthly fatherhood, fatherland, friends, goods, or flesh and blood are as nothing.

So grant us, Father, that we may also be your heavenly children. Teach us to think only of our souls and of our heavenly inheritance, that our material fatherland and earthly life may not deceive and hold and hinder us, making us children of this world. Instead, may we truly say, "Our heavenly Father," and may we be truly your heavenly children. Amen.

— *Martin Luther*

So your name may be glorified, not us

Hallowed be your name. Lord, grant us first to know you rightly and to sanctify, glorify, and praise you in all your works. Your power, wisdom, goodness, justice, mercy, and truth are clearly displayed. May we order our whole lives—our thoughts, words, and actions— so your name may never be blasphemed, but rather honored and praised.

Your kingdom come. Rule us by your word and Spirit so that we submit ourselves more and more to you. Preserve and increase your church. Destroy the works of the devil, and all violence which would exalt itself against you, and all wicked plans devised against your word, until we see the full perfection of your kingdom—in which you are all in all.

Your will be done on earth as it is in heaven. Grant that we all may renounce our own will. Help us to obey without complaint *your* will, which is only good. Show us how to do whatever you call us to, as willingly and faithfully as the angels do in heaven.

Give us this day our daily bread. Provide us with all things necessary for the body, Lord, so we may confess that you are the only fountain of all good. Without your blessing, our best efforts profit us nothing. So we pull our trust away from all creatures and place it alone in you.

And forgive us our debts, as we forgive our debtors. For the sake of Christ's blood, do not credit our sins to us, nor the depravity that always clings to us. As we experience your grace, we may also forgive our neighbor from the heart.

And lead us not into temptation, but deliver us from evil. We are so weak we cannot stand. And as we face ceaseless assaults from our deadly enemies the devil, the world, and even our own flesh, preserve and strengthen us by the power of your Holy Spirit. Then we will not be overcome in this spiritual warfare, but instead may constantly and strenuously resist our foes, until at last we see complete victory.

For yours is the kingdom, the power, and the glory forever. We ask you all this because you are the Almighty, our king. You are more powerful than all enemies, and all things are in your power. We pray so your holy name—not we ourselves—may be glorified forever. Amen.

— *Zacharias Ursinus*

Watch Over Us Every Day

(Prayers for Protection)

YOU ARE MY ONLY HOPE

Guide me in your truth and teach me, for you are the God of my salvation; all day long I wait for you.

O Lord! All who are of the truth hear your voice—the voice of their only shepherd, and the true Bridegroom. But we flee from the voice of a stranger, fearing that we might be deceived.

Remember your afflicted and poor servant, O Lord. You search all hearts. You know that I seek nothing but your will. So direct me to your truth, and teach me. You are the God of my salvation; besides you I acknowledge none other.

You only are my hope, my comfort, my shield, defense, and the fortress upon which I depend with confidence. I wait on you in my fear, misery, tribulation, and need. Amen.

— *Menno Simons*

DO NOT LET ME BE TEMPTED BEYOND WHAT I CAN BEAR

Guard my soul and save me; do not let me be ashamed, for I take refuge in you.

Lord, the words of Paul fill me with terror, where he says, "let anyone who thinks that he stands take heed lest he fall" (1 Corinthians 10:12). And "If anyone thinks he is something, when he is nothing, he deceives himself" (Galatians 6:3).

I ask you therefore, blessed Lord: keep my soul, which is bought with so dear a price, so I never turn from your truth. For though I may now think with Peter that I could give my life for you, or with Paul that neither tribulation, nor life, nor death, nor any other creature will be able to separate me from your love—yet I do not know myself well enough.

All my trust is in you. I have not yet resisted unto blood, though I have tasted a bit of the cup of your affliction. Still I have not tasted the dregs. So when it comes to prisons and suffering, when life or death are threatened, the gold will be separated from the wood, silver from the straw, pearls from the stubble.

Please never leave me, gracious Lord. Trees with the deepest roots are pulled from the earth by the violence of a storm. And lofty, firm mountains are torn apart by the force of an earthquake. But, gracious Lord, do not let me be tempted above what I am able to bear.

I pray not for my flesh. I am well aware that I must once suffer and die. I simply ask that you would strengthen me in the battle. Assist and preserve me. Make a way for me to escape temptation. Deliver me and let me not be ashamed, for I put my trust in you. Amen.

— *Menno Simons*

KEEP ME FROM A FLIMSY GOSPEL

Let integrity and uprightness protect me, for I wait for you.

O Lord, when the farmer planted good seed in his field, his enemy came and sowed weeds. Wherever Jesus is, there will the devil be found near at hand.

So it is with your saving word and your gracious gospel, the proper food for my soul. It has been trampled upon for so many years, called a dead tale or a useless fabrication. But as soon as it is again received and believed in power, the hellish lion roars in rage. He never rests, knowing that his dominion must decline and be destroyed by your word. He makes use of all his cunning and subtlety, and transforms himself into an angel of light. So those whom he has lost through your word he lures back into his snare by false doctrine. Through false prophets and unskilled teachers, he changes the pure, saving sense of the Scriptures into something entirely carnal, calculated to mislead.

But everything you did not plant will come to nothing, Lord. Preserve me pure and upright in your truth, so that I may neither believe nor teach anything that does not conform with your holy will and word. May it always align with true faith, sincere love, a genuine baptism and Lord's supper, and a blameless life.

Preserve me, gracious Lord, from all error and heresy. Help me and my beloved brothers and sisters to seek, love, and fear you with all our hearts. Help us to obey the government in all things not contrary to the word of God.

Preserve us from the wiles of the devil who would want to teach us of another king besides the true King of Zion.

For Jesus Christ alone rules with the iron scepter of your word. He alone is King of kings and Lord of lords. He alone is set at your right hand in the heavenly places, far above all principality and power, above all might and dominion and every name that is named—not only in this world, but also in the one to come.

All things are put under the feet of Christ, who has all power in heaven and on earth, and before whom every knee must bow, and every tongue confess that he is Lord, to the glory of your great name.

Gracious Lord, preserve me under your cross with integrity and uprightness, so that I may not deny you and your holy word in the time of temptation. May I never conceal your divine truth or will under the mask of hypocrisy, lies, or obscure language. And may I receive your promised kingdom and inheritance at the appearance of your Son.

Because of your gracious promise, we hope each day for your reward with firm assurance and perfect confidence. Amen.

— *Menno Simons*

GUARD US ALL OUR DAYS

O Lord, we will bless you all our days, and our souls will glory in your grace. Your praise will dwell on our tongues, while saints and angels will join our songs.

We pray that you will let the heavenly host serve as guardians of our land and coast.

May they watch over your flock of grace, that we may lead a life of peace. Amen.

— *Philip Melanchthon*

LET THE TRUMPET OF YOUR HOLY GOSPEL SOUND!

My Lord, what an abomination! Can the sun shed its beams on such a country? Or can the earth bear such people, and yield its fruits to those who so despise their creator?

And you, O God, are you so compassionate, so slow to wrath and vengeance against those who commit such great wickedness by forbidding the use of the Holy Scriptures, and sin against you?

Have you not appointed your Son as King over all? Will that holy revelation which you have imparted through him for our instruction now be forbidden as a useless or even dangerous document to those who read it?

Arise, O Lord! Show that it is your will that your Son should be honored, and the sacred statutes of his kingdom

should be known and observed by all. Let the trumpet
of your holy gospel sound throughout the world! Grant
strength to all true evangelists, and destroy all those who
promote error, that the whole earth may serve you, and
call on your name with the profoundest adoration! Amen.

— *William Farel*

HELP! THE ENEMY HATES US!

Lord, there is no doubt that we are poor sinners, and by
our disobedience we have deserved infinitely more severe
discipline than we are now bearing. But look, Lord, at the
wicked enemy's intentions.

The enemy hates you and your name, and hates us too
because we hold fast to you and your name, because
we find comfort in your word, and because we hope for
mercy through your death and merits.

Therefore, dear Lord Jesus Christ, punish our enemy, and
help us for your name's sake!

Such a thought cheers our hearts, giving us confidence and
boldness to pour ourselves out to you in prayer. For this
reason the prophets also prayed in this way, constantly
pleading the name of God, as David does: "Yet for your
sake we are killed all the day long; we are regarded as
sheep to be slaughtered" (Psalm 44:22).

Amen.

— *Martin Luther*

WE PRAY FOR PERSECUTED BELIEVERS

Almighty God and merciful Father, we humbly submit ourselves to you. We fall down before you. And we humbly ask that you would grant us your Holy Spirit to direct our prayers, that they would agree with your will.

From the bottom of our hearts, we ask that the seed of your word now sown among us may take such deep root that the burning heat of persecution would not cause it to wither, nor that the thorny cares of life would choke it.

But like the seed sown in good ground, may it bring forth manyfold, whatever you decide in your wisdom.

Since in our weakness we are unable to do anything without your help, and you are well aware of the great temptations that surround us, let your strength sustain our weakness, Lord. When we are defended by the force of your grace, we are preserved against all the assaults of Satan, who roams about like a roaring lion, seeking to devour us.

Increase our faith, merciful Father, so we do not swerve from your word. Build us up in hope and love and help us to carefully keep your commands. May no hardness of heart, hypocrisy, lust of the eyes, or enticements of the world draw us away from obedience to you.

And since we live in such dangerous times, protect us in your fatherly providence against the violence of our enemies, which follows us everywhere.

We pray not only for ourselves, but also for all those who still do not know you. Bring them out of that miserable captivity of blindness and error into a pure understanding and knowledge of your heavenly truth. Then with one consent of unity of minds we may all worship you, our only God and Savior.

We also pray for pastors, shepherds, ministers—all to whom you have entrusted the task of sharing your word. May they be found faithful in life and doctrine, seeing before them only your glory. And may those sheep who wander be gathered and brought back into your fold.

And since the heart of every ruler is in your hands, Lord, direct and govern their hearts. Maintain and increase the honor of our city. Preserve those leaders in your fatherly favor. Govern their hearts, Holy Spirit, in such a way that faith and good conduct will be maintained, and sin put away.

We lift up those who are going through trials—wars, pandemics, famine, sickness, poverty, imprisonment, persecution, or any other trouble—physical or otherwise. Give them patience and help them to endure until you deliver them.

We also lift up our brothers and sisters who are persecuted, thrown in prison, or even executed for their testimony to the truth. Comfort them and inflame their hearts with the Holy Spirit, that they may boldly and cheerfully endure whatever trials you appoint. By death or by life, may the kingdom of your dear Son Jesus Christ increase and shine through all the world.

We bring you these petitions in his name. Amen.

— John Knox

PROTECT YOUR TRUTH IN THIS TROUBLED TIME

Lord, you have helped your church, even from the beginning, and for its deliverance you have plagued cruel persecutors from time to time. Your hand drowned Pharaoh. Your power repulsed the pride of Sennacherib. And your angel so plagued Herod that worms and lice were punishers of his pride.

O Lord, you remain the same forever. Your nature is unchangeable. You hate cruelty, pride, oppression, and murder. And now, even worse, they seek to banish your dear Son Jesus Christ from this realm. They seek to banish the true preaching of his word, as well as his faithful ministers.

Look therefore on us, O Lord, in the multitude of your mercies. Stretch out your arm and declare yourself the protector of your truth. Repress the pride and fury of these cruel persecutors. May they never prevail against us and may they never extinguish the brightness of your word from this realm.

We accept your will for whatever is to become of our bodies. But we humbly pray, for the sake of Jesus Christ, that you would maintain the purity of your gospel, that we and our descendants may enjoy its fruits to the praise and glory of your holy name.

So we ask for your mercy by the merit and intercession of our Lord Jesus Christ, to whom, with you and the Holy

Spirit, be all honor, glory, praise, and blessing, now and forever, so be it.

— John Knox

A QUIET LIFE IN THE MIDST OF PERSECUTION

Most benign and merciful God, we yield to you the greatest and most thanks as we are able.

You have ingrafted us in Christ, your true and natural son—not by the ministry of angels, or of any other creature whatsoever, but by the power of your own Spirit. And through Christ you have renewed and sanctified us, setting us apart.

You have so much enriched us with the knowledge of your son, and with other heavenly gifts. So now we lack neither strength, energy, light, or any ability to will or do what pleases you.

And thus we will live a cheerful and quiet life, even in the midst of persecutions, which often the world and Satan do stir up. And we are most fully persuaded by that Holy Spirit that we will obtain eternal life, and that not of our own merits, but by the grace of our Lord Jesus Christ, which lives and reigns forever, amen.

— Peter Martyr Vermigli

Keep us until that day

O Lord, eternal God and dear heavenly Father, with your Son you have shown us that the skies and the earth will perish, but that we will in our physical bodies rise and so avoid judgment.

Dear Father, we humbly pray that you with your Holy Spirit would shelter us by your word and in a right faith. Preserve our spirits from sin and help us overcome every temptation, that our hearts might be kept and fed in these evil last days.

And may we also awake in godly prayer as we seek your fatherly mercy. So then in safe confidence we may look forward with joy to your Son's return, who with you and the Holy Spirit lives and reigns forever, one true God, amen.

— Hans Tausen

Protect me from your enemies, according to Psalm 139

Deliver me, Lord, from ungodly and arrogant persons. You see how in their hearts they plan trouble, and love to start arguments. Under their lips lurks the poison of a rattlesnake.

God of mercy, do not let me fall into their hands or mistreat me. You alone are my God; hear my cry. You are the strength and power of my defense, whenever I am assaulted. Do not allow the wicked to succeed and to denounce you in their spite.

Look upon my cause and my misfortune. Deliver me!
Then with a right heart and glad assurance I will proclaim
and lift up your holy name. Amen.

— Primer of 1559

IF YOU APPEAR, YOU WILL SCARE
THE DEVIL AWAY

Lord Jesus Christ, through the Apostle Peter you told us
that our "adversary the devil prowls around like a roaring
lion, seeking someone to devour" (1 Peter 5:8).

He is busy and fierce, and if we did nothing, he could soon
deceive us with his craft, overturn us with his might, and
in his cruelty tear us into pieces.

But if you would appear, Lord—even from a distance—you
would frighten him. With just a look you would put him to
flight. You have already overcome.

Receive us into your protection, Lord. We are still only
infants—weak, feeble, and unskilled. The fierce beast
would attack us. So in this fight we lift up your banner: the
cross. The cross, your triumph and victory. We live our
lives by your counsel, aid, and strength. To you be glory
forever. Amen.

— Primer of 1559

WE STAND AGAINST THE DEVIL—
BUT ONLY IN YOUR POWER

Jesus Christ, our Lord God, you are our shield and fortress, our strong rock and our only defense.

You know with how great a force that old enemy of ours comes to assault us. The wily serpent beguiled our first parents in paradise. The roaring lion goes about night and day, seeking victims to devour. The devil is a destroyer and waster, the accuser of the saints.

We have no power at all in ourselves to withstand him. So unless you help us, he will easily deceive us with his craftiness, overthrow us by his strength, and tear us to pieces in his cruelty.

But we also know that you will drive him away with just a look. For you have overcome him by your death. You have bound him. Disarmed him. Ruined his house. You have taken away all his lordship and power. You have crushed his head, cast down his throne, and dispossessed him of his kingdom. You have taken any obligation we had to him, and nailed it to the cross. And you have triumphed over him in our nature.

We are weak, naked, unarmed, unskilled, and ignorant. So we come to you—the strong, almighty, wise one— asking you to defend and preserve us from the merciless dragon. Be our eyes, our ears, and our hands. Be our pilot, our guide, and our captain. Defend us against this adversary. Deny his schemes. Confound his tricks. Break his weapons. Overthrow his holds. Quench his fiery darts.

Chase away his armies and give your servants the upper hand. By us and in us, overcome him and his.

Advance the banner of the cross in our hearts, and you will drive him out of the battlefield. Under this banner we dare to march boldly against him. We know that in your power you will deliver us from our enemies, and all that hate us, so we may serve you in holiness and righteousness all the days of our life.

We ask you this for the sake of your mercy, and to the eternal honor of your holy name, amen.

— *Book of Christian Prayers of 1578*

BEFORE A JOURNEY

Lord, bless this journey, and go with me. Or if you do not carry me, then stop me.
You who guided Abraham's servant by an angel, and the wise men by a star.

You who preserved Peter in the waves, and Paul in a shipwreck.

Be present with me, O Lord, and arrange my path. Go with me, lead me out, and lead me back.

May God arise, may his enemies be scattered, and may those who hate him flee from his presence (Psalm 68:1). I will keep the commandments of my God.

Amen.

— *Lancelot Andrewes*

From an expecting mother
to the author of life

You wisdom and power shine forth in all your works, O Lord. But how much greater, unmistakable, and so much more wonderful are they in the shaping of a human life. From such a small beginning you make so marvelous a living thing, shedding into it a soul whose original is from heaven. So we long to return there, as if back to our own country.

Now that you have agreed to make me, as it were, your workshop—a place to fashion so extraordinary a creation—from my heart I give you my deepest and most humble thanks.

And as you have given me the ability to conceive, I ask that you would also give me the strength to bring to perfection the little life growing in me. May I safely bear and bring forth this child.

And gracious life-builder, in your mercy would you either diminish the coming pain, or else increase my strength and courage to overcome. Amen.

— *Book of Christian Prayers of 1578*

Grant us patience in trouble

Lord, you have humbled me and pulled me down!

For you are angry with me, but I deserved your anger. Clearly I have sinned, Lord. I confess it: I will not deny.

But Lord, please pardon my trespasses, release my debts, and deliver now your grace again unto me.

Care for my wounds, for I am plagued and beaten. Even so, Lord, I turn to you, waiting for your relief. For I have received a token of your favor and grace towards me—the word of promise concerning Jesus Christ, who for me was offered on the cross as a ransom, a sacrifice, and the price for my sins.

Defend me according to your promise, Lord. Defend me in your strength, and in your grace hear my requests. Be my overcomer in perils, for all human efforts are vain. Beat down my enemies with your power, which is my only aid and protection, O Lord God almighty. Amen.

— Primer of 1559

YOU ARE THE WAY

Our life is a pilgrimage, Lord. We came from you, and we make our journey to you. We travel through dark places, on perilous tracks.

Christ, you are our true compass and guide. You are always faithful and friendly. Put out your hand, open my eyes, and make your highways known to me.

You entered first the way out of this corrupt life, and you have fenced a path for us through to eternal life. You are the way. Lead us to the Father by yourself, so we may be one with him, even as you and the Father are one.

Show me the way I should walk, for I lift up my soul to you. Amen.

— John Bradford

A PRAYER FOR CHRISTIAN UNITY, ACCORDING TO PSALM 68

Arise, Lord, and let your enemies be scattered. Put to flight those who hate you.

The righteous and Christ's disciples are celebrating with cheer. Let us sing praises and joyful songs unto you. Let us share how magnificent you are. Let us promote your majesty. Let your glory grow. Let the kingdom of Christ from heaven be enlarged among the chosen.

Lord, be the father of the fatherless and the advocate of the widows. Be the protector of those the world has rejected, those with troubled consciences, those who are pursued for Christ's sake, those whose lives are needy and wrapped in misery.

Let us live in peace and unity in your house, Lord. Give us one heart, one mind, and one true understanding of your word.

Pluck off the chains from the consciences and bodies of the captives—and also of them who are still on the path of death, those who are misguided and still strive against your grace.

Pour down the showers of your grace, Lord. Bring forth fruit, and strengthen your people with your Spirit.

Grant us your word in abundance, so there may be many preachers of your gospel who will work together and agree together. Let your church, the bride of Christ, collect the treasure of saved lives from the conquered Satan.

May all who believe in you through Christ lift you up with praise, celebrating and proclaiming your glory!

We have embarked on the voyage of salvation; bring us safely to port. And when you have delivered us from death, we may escape and come to life. Finish the thing you have begun in us. Make us increase from faith to faith, and do not leave us to our own will and choice, for it is slippery and ready to fall.

Eliminate violence with the thunderbolts of your word, so we may give the glory to you alone. Give to your people the courage and power to withstand sin, and to obey your word in all things, God most glorious and excellent over all. Amen.

— Primer of 1559

I CALL FOR HELP

Christ Jesus, our Lord: Deliver us by your glorious presence. Help us! We are miserable and poor, and we groan for you. We seek you from the heart, according to the grace you have given us, through the influence of the Holy Spirit, who lives and reigns with you and the Father, blessed forever, amen.

— Martin Luther

Look down on us and this small portion of earth

Merciful God, you grant all peace. You are the giver of all good gifts, the defender of all nations. And you desire us to count all people as neighbors, to love them as ourselves, and not to hate our enemies. Rather, you want us to wish them well, and also to do them good if we can.

Look down upon us and see this small portion of earth where the name of Jesus Christ is proclaimed. Give to all of us the desire for peace, unity, and calm. Make us weary of all war and hostility, weary of bitterness toward those we call enemies. May we and they praise your holy name with one heart. May we all remake our lives according to your way.

Grant, O Lord, that our children's children may know the benefit of your great gift of unity. May you discredit all those who work against it. Diminish their strength and punish those who interrupt godly peace—or rather, convert their hearts to the better way, and make them embrace unity and peace, which will be for your glory.

Put away from us all war and hostility. But if we are driven to it, be our shield and protection as we seek peace.

Do not look on our sins, Lord, or the sins of our enemies. Do not give us what we deserve, but remember your abundant, infinite mercy. Do this, O Lord, for your Son's sake, Jesus Christ. Amen.

— *Thomas Cranmer*

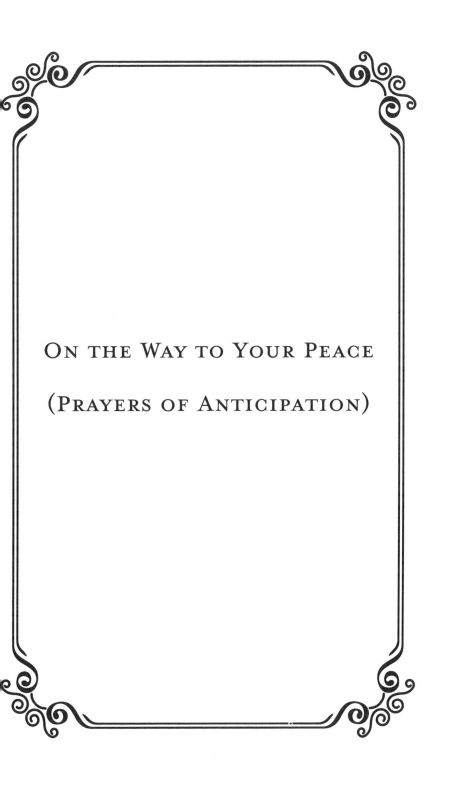

On the Way to Your Peace

(Prayers of Anticipation)

Thank you for my home, my refuge

Lord, nothing is more like your holy nature than a quiet mind. You have called us out of the troublesome turmoil of the world into your quiet rest and peace, which the world cannot give. It is the "peace of God, which surpasses all understanding" (Philippians 4:7).

You ordain homes for us—places where we can get out of the weather and be safe from danger, the unrest of other people, or just from the toils of the world.

I think of what a wonderful return it will be to come to our eternal, most quiet, and most happy home—heaven! Then all grief will be gone away. Whatever is pleasant and joyful here on earth, it will be but a shadow of what is to come.

But now, gracious Father, grant that I may enter my earthly home to be safe from the outside world, and that today I may have godly quiet in body and soul, and peace here to praise you. Amen.

— John Bradford

Help us fight to the end

Almighty God, you fortified your servants the prophets with the invincible power of your Spirit. Now would you make us humble, knowing what they taught—that we may learn to willingly submit before you and so gladly receive and accept what you offer.

Sustain us by your hand so that we rely on your power and protection, so we may be equipped to fight the world and Satan. May we all, in whatever position or job we find ourselves, rest in your power. May we not hesitate to expose our very life to danger, whenever necessary. And with courage may we fight and persevere in our battles to the end.

Then, when we finish our course, we will ultimately come to that blessed rest which is reserved for us in heaven, through Christ our Lord, amen.

— John Calvin

A prayer for the prodigal's brother

Dear Lord: If my brother, who is outside, hears the music and the tune from the feast of peace and concord, and if he trusts in his own strong arms ... but only whispers and grows angry? Then in your great mercy, let him see his blessings.

My own works are nothing. And out of your fatherly kindness, you have pulled me out of the shadows.

So with all the saints, I give you eternal glory, amen.

— Marguerite de Navarre

BRING DOWN WHAT OPPOSES YOUR WORD

Strong and mighty God, you destroy the word of the ungodly and rid the world of tyrants, whenever you decide. No force can resist your everlasting determination.

Now look on your cause for the sake of our Lord and Savior Jesus Christ. It is time, Lord. Bring to nothing all those things that stand against you and your holy word. Do not let the enemies of your truth oppress your word and your servants. We seek only your glory, and above all things wish in our hearts that your holy name would be glorified among the nations.

Grant that we your servants would speak your irresistible truth and wisdom. Even though we justly deserve this plague and famine of your word, we pray that you would release us in our true repentance. We vow before you to better use our gifts, and to order our lives according to your will and pleasure.

We will sing unending praises to your blessed name, world without end, through Jesus Christ our Lord, amen.

— John Knox

Give us strength to overcome

Dear Father, we pray that you would give us first your Word, that the gospel would be sincerely preached throughout the world. And we pray that it would be accepted in faith, to work and to live in us, so that through the word and the power of the Holy Spirit your kingdom may prevail among us to the defeat of the devil's kingdom. May he have no claim and power over us!

Would you utterly overthrow him, so that the power of sin and death and hell may be destroyed, and so we may live forever in perfect righteousness and blessedness.

Your will be done, dear Father, and not the will of the devil or of our enemies, nor of those who would persecute and destroy your word, or prevent your kingdom from coming.

Enable us to bear with patience—and ultimately overcome any suffering because of your kingdom, and so save our poor flesh from falling through weakness or laziness.

Amen.

— *Martin Luther*

WE LIFT UP THOSE WHO NEED
TO KNOW YOU

We come to you, Lord, on behalf of humanity, for those who are not Christians, and for the conversion of those who do not know you. We pray for restoration in the lives of all who are sick in their false beliefs and sins, and for all to whom you will grant truth and grace.

We pray that you would encourage all who are ill and discouraged, all who are in need or unsettled, men and women. We pray for all who are cheerful and healthy; show them how to be thankful.

We pray for the increase of your church worldwide—for deliverance, peace, and unity. Supply what we lack and strengthen what remains.

We pray for all in authority in government. For judges, for those who serve in the armed forces and law enforcement, for farmers and fishers, merchants and mechanics, for workers and the poor.

We lift up the younger generation to you, and those who care about us—even those we do not know. We lift up all who are undertaking any good work which will bring you glory. For all who support the poor. And for all who have ever been offended by me, either in word or in deed.

Have mercy, Lord. Direct my life toward your commandments. Purify my body and soul. Direct my thoughts and cleanse my desires. Renew me thoroughly, O God. For if you want to, you can. Amen.

— Lancelot Andrewes

Help us to never presume on our own strength

Almighty God, you allowed Peter the apostle to fall miserably as he presumed on his own power—not only in denying his master, Christ, in fear of those around him, but also in cursing himself by denying he ever knew the Lord.

Merciful Father, help us to never presume on our own strength. Give us humble and lowly hearts instead. Help us to acknowledge our own condition, frailty, and weakness. May we always be prepared to receive your strength and comfort in order to accomplish well your holy and blessed will.

Hear us, Heavenly Father, for the sake of our Lord Jesus Christ. Amen.

— Primer of 1559

DO NOT LET THOSE WHO DESPISE YOU BE CURSED

O Lord, even as your merciful grace covers all who fear you, so also is your fierce wrath over all who despise you, who chase their own lusts, and who dare to say, "There is no God."

That is a covenant with death, an agreement with hell. To think that God does not know what we do! That we will eat and drink, for tomorrow we die. That our life is short and full of trouble, and there is no hope afterwards. That we should live in affluence while using others. That we can oppress the poor or defraud the righteous.

Dear Lord, the world is so mistaken, living in the lusts of the flesh, the lust of the eyes, and in the pride of life. Wherever we turn, we see deceit, unrighteousness, and tyranny. Few people fear your name.

Paul says that to be carnally minded is death (Romans 8). And the sentence is already passed. The Scriptures teach that if we live according to the flesh we die. If we do not repent there is nothing more certain than fierce anger.

Therefore, dear Lord—threaten, reprove, admonish, and teach. Perhaps some may yet repent, know the truth, and be saved. They are the work of your hands, created in your image, and dearly bought. Do not let them be cursed like Cain, Sodom, or Pharaoh.

Amen.

— *Menno Simons*

MAY I LONG FOR HEAVEN, MY HOME

When we graduate to your blessed presence, and arrive at the safety of immortality and salvation, then we will know no sickness, no need, no pain, and no kind of evil to soul or body. Whatever good we can wish, we will have. And the things we hate will be far from us.

Dear Father, if only we had faith to see things as they really are! If only our hearts were persuaded, and our desires set afire with a desire for the things of heaven. Then we would live in longing for that which we now despise the most.

When we think on death, Lord, our minds are often oppressed with darkness. We only remember the night of the body, forgetting the light of the resurrection.

It is like sailing over the sea to our home and country. Or like the pain of a woman in labor, as the child is delivered into a much greater place than the womb. So our souls are delivered into heaven.

What is this life but a vapor, a shadow, a bubble, a word, grass, a flower? We will certainly die, but no one knows exactly when.

Help us, Lord. Though we are ignorant of things to come, and we do not know the time of our death (but you certainly do), grant that we may finish our journey here and live in such a way that shows we are ready. And then let us depart when it gives you the most glory and our comfort in Christ.

Amen.

— *John Bradford*

Grant us peace as we return home

Lord, how excellent and full of joy it will be to come home into the everlasting quiet and blessed house of heaven, where there are no troubles or burdens.

All the joy and gladness of this world is but a shadow compared to the pleasures there. You have called us into your quietness and peace from out of the turmoil of this world—from out of storms into a haven. It will be a peace the world cannot give, and exceeds all our ability to imagine or create.

Merciful Father, grant now in your unmatched goodness that we may retreat to the safety of our homes, just as we yield ourselves in obedience to you. Houses are built for us to retreat from the weather and from the storms and turmoil of this troubling world. Grant us your peace—the peace of Jesus Christ to this house, and to all who live here. Amen.

—Book of Christian Prayers of 1578

Fix our thoughts on heaven

Almighty God, you have reminded us in your word, and you have taught us by so many examples: There is nothing permanent in this world.

The things which seem the firmest ... tend to ruin and decay. They instantly fall and of themselves vanish away. By your breath you buffet that strength in which people put their trust.

We are subdued and humbled before you. Help us not to rely on earthly things, but raise up our hearts and our thoughts to heaven. Fix there the anchor of our hope, and may all our thoughts abide there.

Then when you have led us through our course on earth we will be gathered into that heavenly kingdom which has been obtained for us by the blood of your only-begotten Son. Amen.

— John Calvin

Give us a sample of heaven's sweetness

Open our eyes, Lord, that we may see the hope to which you have called us. Give us eyes that see, ears that hear, and hearts that understand.

Remember us in your favor, and visit us with your saving health, that we may see the good things you have prepared for your chosen children, that we may catch a glimpse of your heavenly Jerusalem, and that we may have a taste of the sweetness of your house.

Dear Father, kindle in us an earnest desire to be with you in body and soul, and to praise your name forever with all your saints, in your eternal glory, amen.

— John Bradford

Conserve me and keep me as your child

Father, in your mercy you have called me into your family, into the communion of the saints. In that same mercy help me to cry out as do my fellow believers, and desire to be with you—not just because of my present situation, but simply out of love for you.

Write that love in my heart, and graciously hear the words of my mouth—words which I will borrow from the mouths of your servants:

Remember me, O Lord, when you show favor to your people (Psalm 106:4).

Give me the spirit of wisdom and of revelation in the knowledge of him (Ephesians 1:17) and I pray that the eyes of my heart may be enlightened, so I will know the hope of his calling (Ephesians 1:18).

Make me able to comprehend with all the saints what is the width and length and height and depth (Ephesians 3:18) of your sweet mercy. That is, may I know the excellent love of the knowledge of Christ, that I may be fulfilled with all fullness that comes from you.

Enlighten my eyes, or I will sleep the sleep of death (Psalm 13:3), but instead send out your light and your truth (Psalm 43:3) so that I may see the goodness of the Lord in the land of the living (Psalm 27:13).

O give me the Spirit who is from God, so that we may understand the things freely given us by God (1 Corinthians 2:12), those things which no eye has seen, nor ear heard, nor the heart of man imagined, what God has prepared for those who love him (1 Corinthians 2:9).

When will I see the inheritance you keep for me in heaven? When will I hear the sweet voices of the saved people, crying "Salvation belongs to our God who sits on the throne, and to the Lamb" (Revelation 7:10)?

I will do, and I will sojourn, at your pleasure. The timing of my coming into this world was not my choice, but yours. And so you will take me in your mercy not when I will, but when you will.

Meanwhile, conserve me and keep me as your child. And while I am still in this body may I live not in the flesh, but in the Spirit (Romans 8:9), for a small taste of the goodness of your house and sanctuary. May all worldly pleasures grow unpleasant and unsavory, for my eternal comfort through Christ our Lord, amen.

—*John Bradford*

KEEP OUR EYES OPEN, LOOKING
FOR YOUR RETURN

Merciful Father, grant that we would come to know the fullness of that blessed and glorious kingdom of Christ your Son.

Draw our hearts in such a way that we in all obedience would yield ourselves into this kingdom, seeing and paying attention only to those things that are above.

Help us to wholly apply ourselves to spreading that heavenly kingdom far abroad, so it becomes known to all. And instead of attaching all their salvation to things of this world (as many foolish people do in vain) may some turn away from the world to commit body and soul—their whole life—to the only Lord Jesus, the Christ, the only true God.

For it was your pleasure, O God, that in him all perfection should dwell. And that by him all things should be reconciled to you and pacified through his blood, whether in heaven or on earth.

Lord grant us unity and brotherly love in your holy church. Kindle our hearts to fervent and devout prayer. Help us to watch tirelessly and wait deliberately for the coming of your beloved Son. May we never be drunk in excess or physical lust, nor entangled with the snares of this world.

But with the eyes of our heart always open, and praying with upright minds, may we cheerfully meet our Redeemer and live in joy with him forever.

To him be eternal praise and honor. Amen.

— Myles Coverdale

WE LIVE UNTIL THAT DAY

O Heavenly Father, I pray to you for your dear Son's sake, Jesus Christ, our only Savior's sake, that you would reign over us all with your word and your Holy Spirit.

Do not let your enemy's hand have power over us, to steer us away from you. Give the rest of us the will and ability to refute the devil's deeds, adultery, and sexual sin. Make holy all those servants of God's word with your Spirit, so they might learn and seek your holy will.

Help us all that we may live here in the world according to your will—in the fear of God, in honesty, and in pure living—that we may find on the final day of judgment that we are your chosen, in everlasting joy and salvation through your son, our Lord Jesus Christ.

To you, the only good and merciful God, Father, Son, and Holy Spirit, be all worship, honor, and praise forever, amen.

— Niels Hemmingsen

When may I come to be with you?

Lord, you tell us that "In my Father's house are many rooms" (John 14:2). How I long to see that place, where you have prepared an eternal place for me!

"For I am a sojourner with you, a guest, like all my fathers" (Psalm 39:12).

"Few and evil have been the days of the years of my life" (Genesis 47:9), and in my life of exile here I long for my heavenly home, for "our citizenship is in heaven" (Philippians 3:20).

I long to see "the goodness of the Lord in the land of the living" (Psalm 27:13). Our life here is like a prideful show, since "you have made my days a few handbreadths, and my lifetime is as nothing before you" (Psalm 39:5).

"And now, O Lord, for what do I wait" (Psalm 39:7)? Is it not for you? O Lord Jesus, when may I come and appear before you? "As a deer pants for flowing streams, so pants my soul for you, O God" (Psalm 42:1).

What true, perfect, unlimited joy! Joy upon joy! Joy surpassing all joy, without which there is no joy! When will I enter that blessed place of joy, and there behold my God? "As for me, I shall behold your face in righteousness" (Psalm 17:15) and "at your right hand are pleasures forever" (Psalm 16:11).

"They feast on the abundance of your house, and you give them drink from the river of your delights. For with you is the fountain of life" (Psalm 36:8–9).

Amen!

— Johann Gerhard

WE LOOK TO THE RESURRECTION DAY

All-powerful God, most merciful Father, you are the source of continual running fountains of all good graces— they never run dry.

You fashioned our body in our mother's womb, breathing life into a thinking soul. May it come alive while it is joined to the body, and after the death of the body be translated into heaven, there to live in joy and happiness until it returns again into the body being raised from the dead in the last judgment. And then we may rejoice and be glad forever, without end!

To you, God, through Jesus Christ, for whose sake we are made partakers of so great a benefit, be glory, praise, and thanksgiving forevermore, amen.

— Heinrich Bullinger

WE LOOK FORWARD TO GLORY

Dear Father, we pray and we cry with great longing in the Lord's Prayer, "Thy kingdom come."

Help, dear Lord! Speed the blessed day of your second advent, that we may be delivered from the wicked world, from the devil's kingdom, and that we may be released from the awful distress we suffer—inwardly from our own consciences and outwardly from the wicked.

Afflict to the limit these old bodies of ours—so long as we may obtain others not sinful, as these. Bodies not given to iniquity and disobedience. Bodies that can never know illness, persecution, or death. Bodies delivered from all physical and spiritual distress. Bodies made like your own glorified body, dear Lord Jesus Christ.

Thus may we finally realize our glorious redemption, amen.

— *Martin Luther*

HELP US LOOK PAST THE TEMPORARY TO THE ETERNAL

O God, kindle our cold hearts with the fire of faith and love. Help us to earnestly seek you. And when we have found you, may we then fervently receive and keep you, and worship you with a right spirit.

Expel all hardness from our hearts, and anything that is not gentle. Help us to be loving and merciful to the poor. Take from us the terror of all doubt, unbelief, and fear of the world, and comfort us in all adversity.

Grant us the faith of your resurrection. Then, as we look past those things that pass away, we may set all our comfort and hope in the blessed resurrection to come. Amen.

— *Myles Coverdale*

GIVE US GRACE THIS DAY

(MORNING PRAYERS)

A MORNING PRAYER FOR PEACE

Our Heavenly Father, almighty and everliving God, you have brought us to the beginning of this day. So defend us today with your mighty power. Keep us today from falling into sin, and steer us away from danger. May everything we do be aided by your governance, to do always what is righteous in your sight, through Jesus Christ our Lord.

God, you are the author of peace and you want us to live in peace with others. Eternal life comes through knowing you, and whole service to you is perfect freedom. Defend us, your humble servants, against every assault of our enemies, so that we may not fear as we trust in your defense through the might of Jesus Christ.

O Lord, all holy desires, all wisdom, and all just works originate from you. Give now to your servants the peace which the world cannot give. Then our hearts will be ready to obey your commandments, and we may live today in calm assurance and quietness through the merits of Jesus our Savior. Amen.

— *Thomas Cranmer*

TEACH ME THIS DAY TO DO YOUR WILL

Lord God, Heavenly Father, I give you praise and thanks
for protecting me so well this past night. And I ask you,
would you teach me this day to do your will? Protect
me and remind me in all my comings and goings, that in
everything you would be praised and my neighbor lifted
up. Grant your grace and protection to my superiors and
my teachers, my father and mother, my brothers and
sisters, my friends … and everyone! Through our Lord
Jesus Christ, amen.

— *Martin Bucer*

A SHORT PRAYER FOR WHEN I RISE

I give you thanks, heavenly Father, through Jesus Christ
your dear Son, that you have protected me through the
night from all danger and harm.

And now I appeal to you: preserve and keep me this day
also from all sin and evil. I pray that in all my thoughts,
words, and deeds, I may serve and please you.

Into your hands I commend my body and soul, and all
that is mine. Let your holy angel have charge concerning
me, that the wicked one have no power over me. Amen.

— *Martin Luther*

Give us today what we need to serve you

Almighty and merciful God, in your bountiful goodness keep us this day from all things that may hurt us, so that we may be ready both in body and soul, and with free hearts accomplish those things that you would have us do today.

Help us to love the things which you command, and believe what you promise, so that even among the many and different changes in this world our hearts may surely be fixed on your truth.

You know that we live among many and great dangers, and that because of our frailness we cannot always stand up straight. Grant to us the health of body and soul so that by your help we may overcome.

Mortify and kill all those vices in us so that in our conversation our life may express the faith which our tongues confess.

Send your Holy Spirit and pour in our hearts that most excellent gift of love—the bond of peace and all virtues—without which anyone who lives is counted dead. You teach us that all our works without love are worth nothing.

So give us grace to cast away the works of darkness and put on the armor of light. Then when your Son Jesus Christ comes again in his glorious might to judge the living and the dead, we may rise to life immortal, through him who lives and reigns with you and the Holy Spirit, now and forever, amen.

— *Thomas Cranmer*

A PRAYER FOR SUNDAY MORNING

Lord God, Dayspring from on high, in your tender mercy you have visited us. Glory be to you, O Lord. Glory to you!

Creator of the light, you light up the world. The sun's rays are flames of fire, day and night, evening and morning.

You also created invisible light, the light which never sets, that which may be known of God—the Law written in the heart. It is the oracle of prophets, the melody of Psalms, the instruction of Proverbs, and the experience of history.

You are the Lord who has shown us light. Now by your resurrection raise us up to newness of life. Give us strength to repent. God of peace, you raised the great Shepherd of the sheep from the dead through the blood of the everlasting covenant, our Lord Jesus Christ!

You who sent the thrice-holy Spirit down on your disciples, do not withdraw the gift from us. Instead, renew your Holy Spirit within us, day by day.

Father, I dedicate to you my impulses, my intentions, my undertakings—my going out and my coming in, my sitting down and my rising up.

Now make us complete in every good work to do your will. Work in us whatever is pleasing in your sight, through Jesus Christ, to whom be glory forever and ever, amen.

— *Lancelot Andrewes*

I BLESS YOU EARLY IN THE MORNING

O Lord, I will direct my prayer to you early in the morning, and you will see me. I have thought about you when I was waking. You have been my helper.

Blessed are you, O Lord, who created the arch of the skies, the heavens and the heaven of heavens, and all the heavenly powers. You created the angels and archangels, the cherubim and seraphim.

You created the waters above the heavens, all the mists for showers, the dew and hail. You created snow as wool, and frost as ashes, ice as morsels. You bring clouds from afar, the lightning and thunder, the winds and tempests. And you bring the waters for drinking and for bathing.

I bless you, Lord, who made the two lights—sun and moon, the greater and the lesser. You have made the stars for lights, for signs, and for seasons. You have made spring, summer, autumn, winter—days, weeks, months, years—to rule over day and night.

You brought the earth into being and gathered the waters into the sea, with lakes, rivers, and springs. You made herbs and fruit trees sprout. You made the earth, continents, and islands. You made mountains, hills and valleys, meadows and woods. You made green things for food, for enjoyment, and medicine. You made corn and hay, herbs and flowers. You made fruit trees for wine, oil, and spices, and trees for wood. And you made things beneath the earth: stones, metals, minerals.

You are merciful and gracious, always patient and abundant in goodness and truth. You show mercy to many, forgiving iniquity and transgression and sin.

Lord, I will bless you at all times. Your praise will ever be in my mouth. Glory to God in the highest, and on earth peace, goodwill toward all. Amen.

— *Lancelot Andrewes*

A PRAYER AS I WAKE

Lord Jesus Christ, you are the very bright sun of the world, ever rising, never falling. You are the cause of all things. You nourish and preserve. You make joyful all things that are in heaven and earth.

Shine your favor on my spirit, I pray, and drive away the night of sins and mists of errors by your inward light. May I walk all my life without stumbling and offense, pure from the works of darkness and just as appealing as in the daytime.

Grant this, O Lord, who lives and reigns with the Father and the Holy Spirit forevermore. Amen.

— *Primer of 1559*

Preserve my body and soul today

Heavenly Father, you always watch over your faithful people, whether we wake or sleep. You defend and preserve us from not only Satan, but from all other enemies. I thank you that in your fatherly goodness you have taken care of me this past night, and have given me sweet sleep.

In your mercy preserve my body and soul today. May I not think, breathe, speak, or do anything that may displease you, or that may be dangerous to myself or hurtful to my neighbor. I pray that everything I do would be in line with your will, which is always good—and that everything I do would advance your glory and profit my neighbor, whom I ought to love as myself.

And whenever you call me home, may I be found not as a child of darkness, but as a child of light, and so forever reign with you in glory. You are the true and everlasting Light. To you be all honor and glory with your dearly beloved son, Jesus Christ our only Savior, and with the Holy Spirit, amen.

— *Thomas Becon*

Awaken me, body and soul

Dear Father, as you have awakened my body from sleep, so also would you awaken and deliver my soul from the sleep of sin and darkness of this world.

And what is awakened out of sleep, would you also restore to life after death. For death to us is just sleep to you.

Dear Lord, I humbly pray that you would make my body into a minister of godliness to my soul in this present life, so that in the life to come it may take part in the same everlasting joy by Jesus Christ our Lord.

"Awake, O sleeper, and arise from the dead, and Christ will shine on you" (Ephesians 5:14).

Amen.

— John Bradford

CLOTHE ME WITH YOURSELF

Gracious and merciful Savior, Jesus Christ, you know how we are born, clothed and weighed down with the heavy burden of Adam, who fell away thorough disobedience.

Clothe me with yourself, my redeemer and sanctifier. Be my clothing and apparel to keep me warm from the cold of this world. You have yielded yourself obedient in all things to God your Father, to be rid of all lusts of the flesh.

If you are far from me, all things become numb, weak, and stark dead. But if you are here, everything is full of life, right, and strong. So as I wrap my body in these clothes, so clothe me all over—but especially my soul—with yourself. Amen.

— Book of Christian Prayers of 1578

I FOLLOW YOU AS THE SUN RISES

Blessed are you, O Lord our God, the God of our fathers, who turns the shadow of death into the morning and renews the face of the earth. You remove darkness from the face of the night. You banish the night, bring back the day, and bring light to my eyes.

Now blot out my transgressions like a thick cloud. Help me to be a child of light, a child of the day. Help me to walk purely and honestly, as in the day. And keep me this day without sin, but uphold me when I am falling, and lift me up when I am down. Never let me harden my heart to provoke you.

Deliver me today from the snare of the hunter, and from the plague. Guard me against today's evil. Do not let my days be consumed in conceit, or my years in sorrow. Let one day speak to the next; let this day add knowledge to yesterday.

O let me receive your lovingkindness as soon as I wake, for I trust in you. Show me the path to walk, for I lift up my soul to you. Deliver me from my enemies, for I flee unto you.

Teach me to do what pleases you, for you are my God. Let your loving Spirit lead me into a place of right living. Bring me to life, O Lord, for your name's sake, and for the sake of your righteousness rescue my soul from trouble.

Remove foolish thoughts from me, but inspire those which are good and pleasing in your sight. Turn me away from pridefulness, and keep my ears from stooping to hear foolish noise. Wake me early to hear, and open my ears to the instruction of your word.

Place a guard, O Lord, over my mouth and over the door of my lips. Let my words bring out the best in others, seasoned with salt, and only give grace to those who hear.

Let me do something good today, Lord, and spare me according to the greatness of your mercy. Into your hands today I dedicate my spirit, soul, and body—which you have created, redeemed, and regenerated. In your goodness you have given me everything I have.

Guard us from all evil. Guard our souls, I beg you, Lord. Guard us from stumbling, and hold us faultless in the presence of your glory. Guard my going out and my coming in, now and forever. Help me to prosper today, I pray, and grant mercy in the sight of all I will meet.

Save me, O Lord. Hurry to help me. Turn to me and have mercy on your servant today. Amen.

— Lancelot Andrewes

Restore us again to your favor

Almighty God and merciful Father, we do not come before
your majesty trusting in our own merits or worthiness,
but in your many mercies. You have promised to hear our
prayers, which we will make in the name of your beloved
Son, Jesus Christ our Lord.

He has commanded us to gather in his name with the full
assurance not only that he will be among us, but also that
he will be our mediator and advocate, that we may obtain
all those things you deem necessary. So we ask, merciful
Father: turn to us in love and forgive our many sins. We
deserve your wrath and punishment, but receive us to
your mercy for the sake of Jesus Christ. Accept his death
as payment for our offenses. You are pleased in him alone,
and through him you cannot be offended with us.

Seeing how we have made it through the night, so may
we also now spend this day in your service. May our
thoughts, words, and deeds resound to the glory of your
name as an example to all. May others glorify you by
seeing the good works we do.

You have not only created us in your likeness, you have
also chosen us as heirs with Christ of that forever kingdom
which you prepared for us before the beginning of the
world. Increase our faith and knowledge, we pray, and
lighten our hearts with the Holy Spirit. May we live in
godly community with you, and live a life of integrity.

I pray that others may also learn by your Holy Spirit
to believe in you, their only Savior and Redeemer. But

since they cannot believe unless they hear, and they cannot hear except by preaching, and no one can preach unless they are sent, raise up faithful distributors of your mercies, Lord—people who only seek your glory in their life and belief.

Put to shame Satan and his minions, that they may not disturb or confuse your little flock through sects, schisms, heresies, or errors.

And since we have fallen into the latter days and dangerous times, where ignorance has the upper hand and Satan and his ministers seek by any means to quench the light of the gospel, I ask that you protect your cause against the ravenous wolves. Strengthen all your servants, and do not let your patience discourage your children. Do not let our sins hinder your mercies. Consider our trials and the afflictions of our country, which once flourished by your mercy, but now because of contempt for your word is plagued in judgment.

Truly we received more than enough warnings of your vengeance to come, both in your word and in the examples of others. Your people Israel provoked your anger many times through their sins. You punished them in your just judgment. But their sins were never so grievous that you would not receive them to mercy if they returned to you.

So as wretched sinners we earnestly repent of our wickedness and ungodly behavior. Though we cannot ourselves buy a pardon, we humbly beg you, for the sake of Jesus Christ, show your mercy. Restore us again to your favor.

Dear Father, grant us these requests, and all other things we need, according to your promises in Jesus Christ our Lord, in whose name we ask, amen.

— John Knox

LET ME BE DRESSED IN YOUR POWER

Jesus Christ, clothe me with your own self, so that I may never think about how to gratify the desires of the flesh (Romans 13:14), and so I may also cleanly put off all my carnal desires and crucify the kingdom of the flesh in me.

Warm me and keep me from being caught up in the deep freeze of this world. If you are not with me, Lord, everything would be cold, weak, and dead. But if you are with me, all things are warm, fresh, and alive.

So grant as I wrap myself in my coat that you also would clothe me completely with your own self—but especially my soul.

"Put on then, as God's chosen ones, holy and beloved, compassionate hearts, kindness, humility, meekness, and patience" (Colossians 3:12).

Amen.

— John Bradford

I WAKE TODAY TO PRAISE YOU

Glory to you, Lord, glory to you! Glory to you who has given me sleep to strengthen my weakness, and sleep to rebuild my toil-worn body from yesterday's work.

For this day and all days, Lord, place me on your perfect, holy, healthy, sinless course. Send an angel of peace, a faithful guide to camp around me and to suggest what is wholesome.

Grant pardon, Lord, and release me from the penalty of sin and offense.

Grant to our souls what is good, and repentance for the rest of our life, health and peace to the end. And grant peace to the world.

Whatever is true, whatever is honorable, whatever is right, whatever is pure, whatever is lovely, whatever is commendable, if there is any excellence and if anything worthy of praise, Lord, may I think on these things—*and do them.* Amen.

— *Lancelot Andrewes*

You Give, and We Gather

(Mealtime Prayers)

A PRAYER BEFORE MEALS

All things depend on your providence, Lord. You decide when we may receive our food. You give, and we gather. You open your hand, and we are satisfied with all good things.

Heavenly Father, you are the fountain and full treasure of all goodness, the author and giver of all good things. Show your mercies on us your children. Sanctify these gifts that we receive in your merciful generosity. Grant us grace to use them soberly and purely, according to your will.

And above all, may we always remember to seek the spiritual food of your word, for the everlasting nourishment of our souls through Jesus Christ, the true bread of life from heaven. Whoever receives this bread will live forever and reign with you in glory, world without end. So be it.

— John Knox

A SHORT PRAYER BEFORE A MEAL

The eyes of all wait upon you, O Lord, and you give them their meat in due season.

You open your hand and satisfy the desire of every living thing.

O Lord God, heavenly Father, bless us and these your gifts, which we receive from your lovingkindness, through Jesus Christ, our Lord. Amen.

— Martin Luther

A SHORT PRAYER AFTER A MEAL

O give thanks unto the Lord, for he is good, for his mercy endures forever. He gives food to all; he gives to the animals their food, and to the young ravens which cry.

The Lord takes pleasure in those that fear him, in those that hope in his mercy.

We thank you, Lord God, heavenly Father, through Jesus Christ, our Lord, for all your benefits. You live and reign forever and ever. Amen.

— Martin Luther

YOUR PHYSICAL FOOD SUSTAINS, AND SO DOES THE ETERNAL

Dear Lord, with physical food you sustain our daily physical life. Otherwise we would die. And this is surely a great thing, but there is something much greater and more holy: That your grace keeps our souls from dying.

We have much to thank you for in this life. We praise you for prolonging it through your good gifts. But this life is only the way to eternal life.

And so we will not only thank you for things of this earthly life, as best we can, but we also give you eternal thanks for eternal things. Grant to us these desires, for your mercy's sake, amen.

— John Bradford

Help us to share your daily gift of food

Heavenly Father, by your dearly beloved Son Jesus Christ you told us to take no thought for our food, drink, and clothing. You have promised to give us everything we need for our life, if we first seek your kingdom and its righteousness.

So we thank you that in your goodness you have provided us with food today.

Bless now this gift, and give us grace to taste it and always remember you. Help us also never to forget other needy believers. Because as you have been generous and merciful to us, we may in the same way show mercy and kindness to our neighbors by sharing of these your gifts.

Then they and we may with one mouth glorify and with one mind praise your holy name forever and ever, amen.

— Thomas Becon

Waiting on the food that will last forever

Maker and governor of the world, this is a wonderful mystery of your work: that you sustain humans and animals with this food.

Surely the power is neither in the bread nor any other food, but in your will and word—the word by which all things live and have their being. How great a thing it is, that you are able to nourish so many creatures.

David praises you: "The eyes of all look to you, and you give them their food in due season. You open your hand; you satisfy the desire of every living thing" (Psalm 145:15–16).

Without doubt these are wonderful works of your might, Lord!

So I pray to you from my heart, generous and faithful Father: As you bring life to our physical bodies with food, bring our souls to life by the same word, in your grace. Then with body and soul we will praise you until this mortal body puts on immortality, and we will no longer need any other food except you alone. Then you will be our all in all. Amen.

— *John Bradford*

THE BLESSING OF YOUR PRESENCE
AT A MEAL

Lord Jesus Christ, without whom nothing is sweet nor savory, we ask you to bless us and our supper. With the blessing of your presence to cheer our hearts, may we savor and taste of you in all that we eat and drink, to your honor and glory. Amen.

— *Primer of 1559*

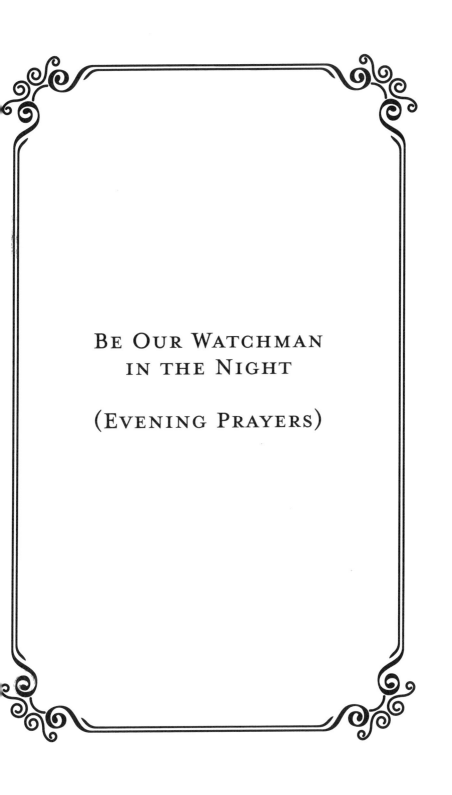

BE OUR WATCHMAN
IN THE NIGHT

(EVENING PRAYERS)

IN THE EVENING OF LIFE
I LIFT MY HANDS TO YOU

The day is gone, O Lord, and I give you thanks.

And as day has its evening, so also has life. The evening of life is age, and age overtakes me. Make the evening bright unto me.

Cast me not away in the time of age. Do not leave me alone when my strength fails me. Even in my old age carry me and deliver me.

Stay with me, Lord, for it is toward evening, and the day is far spent of this toil-worn life. Let your strength be made perfect in my weakness.

Day is fled and gone, and life too is going as night comes, and death. So near as is the end of day, so too the end of life. So we ask you, Lord, O Lord, for the close of our life, that you would direct it in peace. Grant, O Lord, a Christian finish to this life—sin and shame removed, and—if it pleases you—without pain.

Gather us together under the feet of your elect, whenever you will, and however you will—only without shame and sin. Give me the good answer at the dreadful and fearful judgment seat of Jesus Christ our Lord, amen.

By night I lift up my hands to the holy place, and praise you, Lord. You grant your lovingkindness in the daytime. And in the night season will I sing of you, and make my prayer unto the God of my life. As long as I live will I magnify you and lift up my hands in your name.

Let my prayer rise in your sight as the incense, and let the lifting up of my hands be an evening sacrifice.

You are blessed, O Lord, our God, the God of our Fathers, who has created the changes of days and nights. You give songs in the night, and you have delivered us from the evil of this day. You have not cut off my life, from morning even to night. Amen.

— *Lancelot Andrewes*

DEFEND ME FROM THE PERILS AND DANGERS OF THIS NIGHT

I give thanks unto you, heavenly Father, through Jesus Christ your dear Son, that you have so graciously protected me today. And I appeal to you: forgive me all my sins, and the wrong which I have done.

And by your great mercy defend me from all the perils and dangers of this night. Into your hands I commend my body and soul, and all that is mine. Let your holy angel have charge concerning me, that the wicked one have no power over me. Amen.

— *Martin Luther*

A PRAYER AS I FALL ASLEEP

For my weariness, O Lord, grant me rest. For my exhaustion, renew my strength. Give me healthy sleep to pass through this night without fear.

Keeper of Israel, you never slumber or sleep. Guard me this night from all evil. Guard my soul. Reveal to me wisdom in the visions of the night. But if not (for I am not worthy), at least let sleep be to me a breathing time from toil and sin.

In my dreams do not let me imagine anything that would anger you or defile me. Preserve me from the black sleep of sin, and put to sleep within me all earthly and evil thoughts.

Lord, unseen enemies stay awake, and my flesh is so feeble. But you made me. Shelter me under the wings of your compassion. Awaken me at a time when you may be found, at the time of prayer, and let me seek you early, for your glory and service.

I lift up the church to you, Lord. And I pray for leaders in this country, in my community and beyond. I lift up judges and those who serve in the military and law enforcement, farmers and those in business, artists, workers, and the poor.

I lift up all those whose lives intersect with my own, from family and friends to those in the neighborhood.

I place myself in your hands, Lord—body, spirit, and soul. You made and redeemed me, God of truth. Guard my lying down and my rising up, now and forever. Search my spirit. And let me wake to be present with you. I lay down in peace to rest, for you only are the one who makes me live in safety.

Amen.

— *Lancelot Andrewes*

ABIDE WITH US AS EVENING FALLS

Lord Jesus Christ, abide with us as the evening falls. Never let the light of your word be veiled from us in darkness.

Sin's dreaded works abound, and we find no rest as the spirit of falsehood spreads. Error boldly rears its head.

Your church is sluggish, thoughtless, and cold. Prosper your word of grace, and spread its truth. Keep us steadfast in these days of sore distress.

Hold back the deception and rage of Satan. Give us unity, patience, courage, and peace. May your mercy never cease.

Keep us in your word; it is our armor, shield, and sword. Help us confide in its power, and seek no other guide. Amen.

— *Nicolaus Selnecker*

Preserve me as I sleep

O Lord, our keeper and defender, I am unable to defend myself as I lay myself down for the night. I am helpless.

Preserve me now from the schemes and assaults of the enemy.

And grant also that when I have run the race of this life, you would call me in your mercy. Grant that I would live and be with you forever.

My watchman and keeper, take me into your care. Grant that as my body sleeps, my mind may still keep watch in you, and find joy by some vision of that life in heaven where you are King and Prince, together with the Holy Spirit.

Purify my soul and keep clean my body, that in both I may please you, sleeping or waking, forever.

And now, gracious God, let me rest in you. May I not be separated from you, even in sleep. Even in my dreams, draw me closer to yourself, so both my body and soul may be kept pure and holy forever, amen.

—*John Bradford*

Drive away the dimness

Thick, dark clouds cover our minds, Lord, unless your light drives them away.

Your sun is like a spotlight to the world. And your wisdom—light for body and soul—is a spotlight to the spiritual world.

When day is done and the night comes, we can light a candle to chase away darkness. When sin comes, to chase away ignorance, you have given us your truth—which your Son has brought us.

You, the author and master of all truth, are the true light. Make us see, so the dimness of our minds may be completely driven away.

Lift up the light of your face upon us, Lord (Psalm 4:6) and send joy and gladness into our hearts.

Your word is a lamp to my feet and a light to my path (Psalm 119:105).

Amen.

— *John Bradford*

KEEP US FROM FALLING ASLEEP IN SIN

O Lord, maker of all things, this evening we pray that in your mercy you would defend us from every deceit of our enemy. Shield us from being deluded—even in our dreams.

Keep our heart awake in you, and keep us from falling asleep in sin.

Father, please grant this through your blessed Son, to whom with the Holy Spirit be always honor and praise, amen.

— *Primer of 1559*

LET MY HEART NEVER STOP WATCHING YOU

Lord, you are the only God, true, gracious, and merciful. You command those who love your name to cast all fear and worry on you.

In your mercy you promise that you yourself will protect us from our enemies. You promise also to be our refuge in danger, our commander in the day, our light in darkness, and our watchman in the night. You never sleep, but watch continually to preserve your faithful ones.

In your bountiful goodness, Lord, I pray that you will forgive me wherever I have offended you today. Receive me under your protection this night, so I may rest quietly in body and soul.

Grant my eyes sleep, but let my heart never stop watching you—so my weak flesh will not cause me to offend you.

Let me always feel your goodness toward me, so I will at all times be inspired to praise you. May praise be in my mouth late and early and at midday. And at midnight, teach me your judgments, so I may be led in holiness and purity all my life, and I may be inducted finally into the everlasting rest you have promised in your mercy to those who obey your word.

Lord, to you be honor, praise, and glory forever. Amen.

— *Primer of 1559*

KEEP MY TONGUE AND LET ME TRUST IN YOU ALONE

I cry to you, Lord. Hear me now! Let my prayer be a sweet taste in your presence as I lift my hands as an evening sacrifice.

Lord, post a guard by my mouth. Keep watch on my lips and tongue. May I call to you with purity and from the heart as I praise you.

Keep my heart from evil desires, and do not allow me to follow the path of sin or hide my wickedness.

Do not let me live as the world lives, but rather in a way that pleases you. May I never follow the world's advice or lifestyles—including those with a false religious façade. May I never succumb to the enticements and sweet bait of the ungodly, which would draw me into filthy and unclean living. Rather, help me to listen well to those who are genuinely righteous and godly, even if they must sharply correct me.

Let me always pay attention to you alone, to trust in you and apply myself to you. Do not cast away my soul or allow me to perish. Keep and protect me so I am not tangled up in ungodly snares. Save me from the secret traps of the malicious. Defend me in your grace, Lord, because I can never rely on my own efforts. Amen.

— Primer of 1559

Notes

1   Heinrich Bullinger, *Fiftie Godlie and Learned Sermons, Divided Into Five Decades: Containing the Chiefe and Principall Points of Christian Religion, Written in Three Several Tomes or Sections,* (London: Ralph Newberie, 1587), decade 4, sermon 10.

2   Myles Coverdale, *Writings and Translations of Bishop Coverdale,* ed. George Pearson (Cambridge: Cambridge University Press, 1844), 335.

3   Martin Luther, "The Lord's Prayer," in *Works of Martin Luther,* volume 2 (Philadelphia: A. J. Holman Company, 1915), 374–75.

4   Dying prayer of John Calvin's wife Idelette, as quoted by Calvin in a letter to his friend William Farel (who had married them) on April 2, 1549. From Philip Schaff, ed., *History of the Christian Church, vol. VIII* (Ann Arbor, Michigan: Charles Scribner's Sons, 1910), 418.

Biographies and Sources

Henry Airay (1560–1616)

Henry Airay rose from humble beginnings. His father was a servant to the well-known Bernard Gilpin, who generously agreed to finance Henry's early schooling. After Gilpin died, however, Airay apparently was left to work his way through the remainder of his studies at Queen's College, Oxford. At age nineteen he was serving as *pauper puer serviens*, a poor student working out his tuition by attending to the needs of other students during mealtimes, in their rooms, and elsewhere. He did excel in his studies at Queens, however, and was eventually hired as provost and then vice-chancellor. As a pastor and theologian he became known for his fiery sermons defending England's Reformation church and values.

Sources Quoted

Lectures upon the whole Epistle of Saint Paul to the Philippians (Edinburgh: James Nichol, London: James Nisbet and Co., Dublin: G. Herbert, 1864).

Lancelot Andrewes (1555–1626)

As an Anglican pastor and scholar, Lancelot Andrewes served as Bishop of Chichester, Ely, and Winchester. He helped oversee the translation of the King James Version of the Bible, a landmark achievement that would influence the way English-speaking Christians would read the Scriptures for many generations. Andrewes was known as an outstanding scholar who would dedicate a month each year to learning new languages. His devotional literature lives on today. Well-known English composer John Rutter set some of his words to a beautiful choral arrangement, and the prayers in this book are largely adapted from his devotional classic, *The Private Devotions of Lancelot Andrewes, D.D.* He is memorialized today in several English cathedrals, including Winchester, Chester, and Southwark.

Sources Quoted

> *The Private Devotions of Lancelot Andrewes, D.D.*, edited and revised by Edmund Venables (London: Suttaby and Co., Amen Corner, 1883).

THOMAS BECON (1511–1567)

Like many other reformers of the time, Thomas Becon was initially ordained in the Catholic tradition, but broke away when he became convinced of Lutheran teachings. He was arrested for preaching Protestant ideas around 1540, after which he took on a pen name, Theodore Basille. When Edward VI succeeded Henry VIII as king of England in 1547, Becon felt free to preach again, until Mary I came to the throne in 1553. At that time, Becon was arrested again and held in the Tower of London for at least six months. He fled the country after being released, taught in Germany for a time, and returned to England after Elizabeth I came to power. In all that time as a preacher and theologian, Becon's focus was making faith accessible to common people. As he once wrote, "In all my sermons and writings I have not attempted matters of high knowledge and far removed from the common sense and

capacity of the people, but I have been content at all times
to handle such matters as might rather edify the brethren,
than to drive them into an admiration or stupor at the
doctrine of so rare ... high, and unsearchable mysteries."

Sources Quoted

> *Prayers and Other Pieces of Thomas Becon*, edited by John
> Ayre (Cambridge: The University Press, 1843).

THEODORE BEZA (1519–1605)

Theodore Beza was a French Calvinist theologian and
scholar who lived most of his life in Geneva and succeeded
John Calvin as the leader of the Protestant community
there. Well educated in France, he originally studied and
practiced law, but moved on to Geneva after a severe
illness led to a spiritual encounter with and conversion
to Christ. As a talented writer, he caught the attention
of Calvin, and soon became deeply involved in the
Reformation movement there. He died in Geneva at age
eighty-six after decades of helping to guide the fledgling
Protestant church.

Sources Quoted

> *Job: Expounded by Theodore Beza* (Cambridge: John
> Legatt, 1589).

GEORG BLAUROCK (1491–1529)

Though he started his ministry as a Catholic priest, Swiss-
born Georg Blaurock (a nickname meaning "Blue Coat")
arrived in Zürich in 1524 and became one of the founders

of the Anabaptist movement. He worked there for several years with some of the more radical followers of Huldrych Zwingli, most of whom met secretly in homes. He was expelled from Zürich by civic authorities in 1527, and went on to lead and found churches in the Tyrol region of Germany. He was eventually arrested, tortured, and burned alive, but not before leaving a letter and two hymns, all written during his final three weeks. The hymns are included in the venerable *Ausbuch* hymnal and still sung by the Amish. An edited version of his prayer, apparently also written during imprisonment, is included in this collection.

Sources Quoted

> *Martyrs Mirror,* by Thielem J. van Braght, translated by Joseph F. Sohn (Elkhart, Indiana: Mennonite Publishing Co., 1886).

A BOOK OF CHRISTIAN PRAYERS OF 1578, COLLECTED OUT OF THE ANCIENT WRITERS

First published in 1569, *A Booke of Christian Prayers* was also popularly known as *Queen Elizabeth's Prayer Book.* It was published by one of England's leading and most skilled printers of that time, John Daye, who specialized in Reformation-themed literature and who also published *Foxe's Book of Martyrs.* Edited by John's son Richard, the 1578 version was an update of the original, and included several elaborate woodcut illustrations. The subtitle described it as "collected out of the auncie[n]t writers, and best learned in our tyme, worthy to be read with an earnest mynde of all Christians, in these daungerous and troublesome dayes, that God for Christes sake will yet still be mercyfull vnto vs."

Sources Quoted

> *A Book of Christian Prayers of 1578*, edited by Richard
> Daye (London: John Daye, 1578). Reprinted in
> *The Private Prayers of the Reign of Queen Elizabeth*
> (Cambridge: The Parker Society and University
> Press, 1851).

JOHN BRADFORD (1510–1555)

Before switching to law studies, John Bradford originally
began building a successful career as an accountant and
army paymaster. His life changed dramatically, however,
when he came to faith through the witness of a fellow
student. He went on to study theology. After graduation,
"Holy Bradford," as he was known, was noted for his
heartfelt preaching, and was appointed chaplain to King
Edward VI. He preached to all who would listen, all over
London, until his Protestant views eventually placed
him at odds with Queen Mary I. Charged with "Trying
to stir up a mob," he was imprisoned in the Tower of
London, where he studied the New Testament with other
imprisoned reformers, including Archbishop Thomas
Cranmer. Watching other convicted prisoners being
marched to their deaths, he is credited with the phrase,
"There but for the grace of God go I." Bradford was finally
burned at the stake for his faith in July of 1555. In his final
moments, he offered forgiveness to any who had wronged
him, and told the prisoner beside him to "Be of good
comfort, brother, for we shall have a merry supper with
the Lord this night."

Sources Quoted

> *The Writings of John Bradford*, edited for the Parker Society by Aubrey Townsend (Cambridge: The University Press, 1848).

Martin Bucer (1491–1551)

Though not as widely known today as Calvin or Luther, Martin Bucer played an important role as a reformer, pastor, and scholar—primarily in Strasbourg. The son of a cobbler, Bucer excelled in his studies. He also heard Luther speak in 1518, and as a young friar soon received a release from his Dominican vows. He became a pastor and married a former nun, wrote extensively, and worked for reform in Strasbourg and beyond. With Johannes Sturm, he helped turn a Strasbourg Latin school into a seminary, and worked to educate young people in Reformation principles. In his last years, Bucer worked with Thomas Cranmer to revise the *Book of Common Prayer* in England.

Sources Quoted

> *Katechismus von 1537, Martin Bucers Deutsche Schriften* (Band 6,3), *Martin Bucers Katechismen aus den Jahren 1534, 1537, 1543* (Gütersloh: Publikationsreihe de Forschungsstelle der Heidelberger Akademi der Wissenschaften, 1987).

Heinrich Bullinger (1504–1575)

This Swiss reformer succeeded Huldrych Zwingli as senior pastor and leader of the Zürich church. He is known for coauthoring the landmark *Helvetic Confessions*, and served as one of the most important theologians of his time. He originally studied at the University of Cologne just as the controversy arose around Luther's ninety-five theses, and he embraced Lutheran ideas after reading Luther, Melanchthon, and Erasmus. By that time, even his father, a Catholic priest, became a Protestant. Bullinger went on to pastor at a Reformed church and married a former nun. They had eleven children together, many of whom followed their father (and grandfather) to become Protestant pastors. While in Zürich, Bullinger published his popular *Decades*, a series of sermons from which his prayers in this book derive. Though he ultimately had a hard time finding common ground with Lutherans and Anabaptists, he became one of the best-known Reformed thinkers in Europe by the time he died.

Sources Quoted

Fiftie Godlie and Learned Sermons, Divided Into Five Decades: Containing the Chiefe and Principall Points of Christian Religion, Written in Three Several Tomes or Sections, by Heinrich Bullinger (London: Ralph Newberie, 1587).

JOHN CALVIN (1509–1564)

Calvin was born in Noyon, France to a staunch Roman Catholic family, and was expected to become a priest. He began his theological studies in Paris, but moved on to Orleans in 1528 to study law. During that time, he began reading reform-minded books, made reform-minded friends, and is thought to have experienced a sudden conversion experience in 1533, just after graduating. Under a variety of names, he traveled about France, studied, preached, and wrote the first edition of his bestselling *Institutes of the Christian Religion.* At the urging of Reformer William Farel, he ended up in Geneva, where he preached, wrote, and lectured. His prayer at the opening of most of his lectures helped define his decades-long ministry in Geneva: "May the Lord grant that we may engage in contemplating the mysteries of his heavenly wisdom with increasing devotion, to his glory and to our edification." John Calvin indelibly influenced the Reformation movement until his death in 1564.

Sources Quoted

Commentaries on the Book of Prophet Daniel, translated by Thomas Meyers (Edinburgh: Calvin Translation Society, 1852).

Commentaries on the Book of the Prophet Jeremiah and the Lamentations, translated by John Owen (Edinburgh: Calvin Translation Society, 1851).

Commentaries on the Twelve Minor Prophets (Zechariah and Malachi), translated by John Owen (Edinburgh: Calvin Translation Society, 1849).

Commentaries on the Twelve Minor Prophets (Hosea), translated by John Owen (Edinburgh: Calvin Translation Society, 1846).

Commentaries on the Twelve Minor Prophets (Jonah, Micah, Nahum), translated by John Owen (Edinburgh: Calvin Translation Society, 1849).

Commentaries on the Twelve Minor Prophets (Joel, Amos, Obadiah), translated by John Owen (Edinburgh: Calvin Translation Society, 1849).

MYLES COVERDALE (1488–1569)

Several times exiled, Myles Coverdale was one of the earliest and most significant English Reformers. Though ordained an Augustinian friar in 1514, he served under Robert Barnes, who was ultimately burned at the stake for holding Lutheran views. By 1528, Coverdale had left the Augustinians; when he began preaching Protestant ideas, he was forced to flee to the Continent. For the next several years he helped William Tyndale translate the New Testament into English, and completed his own Bible translation in 1535—the Coverdale Bible, known as the first complete English Bible in print. He would also have significant input and influence on many other Bible translations at the time. Returning to England in 1547 when Edward VI became king, Coverdale was appointed chaplain to the Queen Dowager and made a bishop in 1551. However, he was forced to flee England once again when Mary ascended to the throne in 1553. He spent time in Denmark under the protection of the Danish king, then traveled to Geneva, until Queen Elizabeth took the throne in 1558. He never officially reclaimed his role as a bishop, but remained active in the reformed English church, and always signed his name "Myles Coverdale, quondam Exoniensis ("formerly of Exeter"). He died at age eighty-one.

Sources Quoted

Writings and Translations of Bishop Coverdale, edited by George Pearson (Cambridge: The University Press, 1844).

THOMAS CRANMER (1489–1556)

Thomas Cranmer is considered one of the primary architects of the English Reformation. He first made contact with Swiss Reformer Simon Grynaeus, and soon befriended others during an eye-opening tour of Europe. He even married the niece of notable German Reformer Andreas Osiander. Then, serving as Archbishop of Canterbury under Henry VIII, Edward VI, and Mary I, he helped put into writing the new English church's theology and liturgy, and himself wrote early editions of the *Book of Common Prayer.* Later he worked with Martin Bucer on revisions. Unlike his contemporary, Myles Coverdale, who escaped to the Continent when Mary I came to power, Cranmer was imprisoned, tried for heresy, and ultimately executed.

Sources Quoted

The Booke of the Common Praier and Administration of the Sacramentes, edited by Thomas Cranmer (London: Richard Grafton, 1549).

Miscellaneous Writings and Letters of Thomas Cranmer, edited by John Edmund Cox (Cambridge: The University Press, 1846).

A Short Instruction Into Christian Religion: Being a Catechism Set Forth by Archbishop Cranmer in 1548, translated from the original version of Justus Jonas (Oxford: The University Press, 1829).

Elisabeth Cruciger (1500–1535)

Elisabeth Cruciger is known for her early Reformation hymn writing; in fact, she was the first female Lutheran hymn writer. She was born in 1500 in the Pomeranian town of Meseritz (now Poland). A former nun, she heard the preaching of Johannes Bugenhagen and left the Catholic Church in 1521 with her parents. Fleeing to Wittenberg, she eventually married one of Martin Luther's students, Caspar Cruciger. She wrote "Herr Christ, der einig Gotts Sohn" (Lord Christ, God's Only Dear Son), which was included in the *Erfurt Enchiridon* of 1524—one of the original Lutheran hymnals. She died young, at age thirty-five.

Sources Quoted

> *Erfurt Enchiridion*, 1524, in *The Free Lutheran Chorale-Book*, translated by Christopher Neuendorf (Davenport, Iowa: 2015).

John Downame (1571–1652)

Though John Downame came a bit later to the Reformation, he made a lasting impression in his writings and especially in the many works he edited. As a pastor and the son of a bishop, he himself wrote about spiritual warfare, Christian living, treatment of the poor, and how to celebrate communion. His best-known work was called *The Christian Warfare.* Later in life he was also active in ordaining other ministers, as well as serving as a "licenser of the press," granting approval to theological works.

Sources Quoted

> *The Christian Warfare Against the Devil, World, and Flesh* (London: William Stansby, 1634).

> *A Brief Concordance to the Bible* (London: 1631).

GUILLAUME (WILLIAM) FAREL (1489–1565)

Raised in alpine France and educated in Paris, Guillaume Farel in his early years taught grammar and philosophy at the College Cardinal Lemoine in Paris. He was eventually promoted to college regent and worked with reform-minded Catholics there. When he began promoting unwelcome Lutheran ideas (especially against the use of images in worship), he fled Catholic France to Switzerland, where he spent time with Huldrych Zwingli, Martin Bucer, and John Calvin. Fiery, forceful, and known for his thunderous extemporaneous preaching, he was frequently at the forefront of anti-Catholic controversy. Besides his fearless efforts against idols, icons, and relics, he was also known for having a great influence on his friend Calvin, and for convincing Calvin to stay and minister in Geneva.

Sources Quoted

> *The Life of William Farel, the Swiss Reformer,* by Melchior Kirchhofer (London: The Religious Tract Society, 1837).

ANNA OF FREIBURG (?–1529)

Little is known about the life of this convert to Christianity, other than that she was apprehended by authorities in Freiburg, Switzerland, and executed by drowning for her Anabaptist testimony. Her body was subsequently burned as a sort of "double execution." While her influence on the Reformation movement at the time may have been limited, she represents a greater tide of believers during those years who were willing to die for their faith, and her parting prayer has survived through the centuries.

Sources Quoted

> *Martyrs Mirror,* by Thielem J. van Braght, translated by Joseph F. Sohn (Elkhart, Indiana: Mennonite Publishing Co., 1886).

JOHANN GERHARD (1582–1637)

Known as one of the most prominent and exacting theologians of the Reformation, Johann Gerhard was also a popular college lecturer and devotional writer. He also was no stranger to adversity; he barely survived the bubonic plague as a young man, and his first wife died just three years into their marriage. His life was a study in contrasts, as he apparently and often pivoted from writing devotional texts to lengthy (and detailed) theological treatises. During the course of his career he was sought as a professor by nearly every university in Germany, and at the time was considered Germany's greatest living theologian.

Sources Quoted

> *Johann Gerhard's Sacred Meditations,* translated by C.W. Heisler (Philadelphia: Lutheran Publication Society, 1896).

LADY JANE GREY (1537–1554)

Queen of England for just nine days, young Lady Jane
Grey was the victim of tangled political intrigue and
anti-Protestant feelings during the turbulent years of
the English Reformation. In his will, Edward VI had
nominated Jane for the crown, since his half-sister Mary
was a Catholic. But soon after Edward's death, the Privy
Council suddenly proclaimed Mary queen, deposing Jane
and placing her in a precarious position. Her supporters
discredited, she was convicted of high treason under the
subsequent rule of Mary I, and was beheaded in February
of 1554. Jane spoke and wrote Latin and Greek, and
was proficient in French, Hebrew, and Italian. She was
a committed Christian and corresponded with Heinrich
Bullinger. She was only a teen when she was executed, but
has been seen as a martyr for centuries. She recorded the
prayer in this volume just before her death.

Sources Quoted

> *Memoirs and Remains of Lady Jane Grey,* by Nicholas
> Harris Nicolas (London: Henry Colburn and Richard
> Bentley, 1831).

NIELS HEMMINGSEN (1513–1600)

Though nearly twenty years younger than another
influential Danish theologian and pastor (Hans Tausen),
Niels Hemmingsen also made a large impression on the
new Reformation movement in Europe. Like Tausen,
his world was changed after studying in Wittenberg, and
particularly by the teachings there of Philip Melanchthon.
Back in Denmark, he enjoyed influence as a pastor, a
professor at the University of Copenhagen, an advisor to

the king, and a promoter of the Danish school system.
Among other writings, he was known for publishing a
landmark text presenting scriptural arguments against
demonology, witchcraft, and superstition. In his later years
he maintained an ongoing but amiable debate with James
VI of Scotland about several theological issues, including
double predestination.

Sources Quoted

> *The Way of Lyfe: Nicolas Hemmingius (Niels
> Hemmingsen),* translated by N. Denham (London:
> Richard Jones, 1578).

> *On Marriage (Om Ægteskab)* by Niels Hemmingsen,
> portion translated by Robert Elmer (Copenhagen: Mads
> Wingaard, 1572).

BALTHASAR HUBMAIER (1480–1528)

Born in Bavaria and educated at the universities of
Freiburg and Ingolstadt, Balthasar Hubmaier was one of
the most influential and respected Anabaptist leaders of
his generation. Like many others, he began his career as
a committed Catholic, and only later became a Reformer.
Throughout the 1520s, his Anabaptist views began to
make him enemies—notably Prince Ferdinand of Austria.
Hubmaier also disagreed with Zwingli, who at one point
had him arrested. After living and preaching for a time
in Switzerland, he journeyed to Nikolsburg in Moravia,
where he was seized by Austrian authorities and taken
to Vienna. There he was tried and convicted of heresy
(mainly for his rejection of infant baptism), then burned
to death. His wife was drowned in the Danube River three
days after his own execution.

Sources Quoted

"A Forgotten Hymn," in *Balthasar Hübmaier: The Leader of the Anabaptists,* by Henry Vedder (New York: G.P. Putnam's Sons, 1905).

"Twelve Articles of Christian Belief," in *Balthasar Hübmaier: The Leader of the Anabaptists,* by Henry Vedder (New York: G.P. Putnam's Sons, 1905).

"On the Sword," in *Balthasar Hübmaier: The Leader of the Anabaptists,* by Henry Vedder (New York: G.P. Putnam's Sons, 1905).

JOHN KNOX (1514–1572)

Today's Presbyterians have John Knox to thank; he was the founder of the Presbyterian Church of Scotland, and a leader in the Reformation there. Born into a farming family, early on he served as a bodyguard to George Wishart, the traveling preacher who was one of the first reformers in Scotland. After Wishart was burned at the stake, Knox took up the cause to become one of the most influential (and fiery) preachers of his day. At one point he was captured and forced to serve as a galley (rowing) slave, but later continued his ministry in England. During Queen Mary's Catholic reign, he fled to Switzerland to study under John Calvin. He returned to Scotland in 1559 to lead the Scottish Reformation movement. He preached his final sermon on November 9, 1572, and died five days later.

Sources Quoted

  The Works of John Knox, collected and edited by David
  Laing, volume 4 (Edinburgh: James Thin, 1895).

MARTIN LUTHER (1483–1546)

Others before Martin Luther questioned the practices
and corruption of the church, but his ninety-five theses
posted to the door of the Wittenberg church in 1517 lit the
fuse for change. Luther was born in 1483 and ordained
to the priesthood in 1507. And though he is perhaps
best known for his opposition to church practices like
indulgences, his hymns and his translation of the Bible
into vernacular German also made a big impact on both
the church and his culture. He taught that salvation is a gift
of God through grace, and was excommunicated by Pope
Leo X in 1521. He married the former nun Katharina von
Bora after helping to smuggle her out of her convent in
1523. Together they had six children. He delivered his last
sermon in February of 1546, only days before his death.
But the movement he had ignited had only just begun. In
Luther's last statement (found on his body after his death),
he wrote: "We are beggars. This is true."

Sources Quoted

  "Luther's Small Catechism," in *Luther's Catechetical
  Writings,* volume 1, translated by John Nicholas Lenker
  (Minneapolis: The Luther Press, 1907).

  "Brief View and Order of all Seven Prescribed Petitions:
  A Dialog Between the Soul and God," in *Luther's
  Catechetical Writings,* volume 1, translated by John
  Nicholas Lenker (Minneapolis: The Luther Press, 1907).

The Table Talk of Martin Luther, translated by William Hazlitt (London: Bell & Daldy, 1872).

Thirty-Four Sermons on the Most Interesting Doctrines of the Gospel (Glasgow: John Bryce, 1767).

"Whether Soldiers, too, Can Be Saved," in *Works of Martin Luther*, volume 5 (Philadelphia: A.J. Holman Company and Castle Press, 1931).

Luther's Correspondence and Other Contemporary Letters, volume 2, edited by Preserved Smith and Charles M. Jacobs (Philadelphia: The Lutheran Publication Society, 1918).

"Instructions on Confession," in *Luther's Catechetical Writings,* volume 1, translated by John Nicholas Lenker (Minneapolis: The Luther Press, 1907).

"The Lord's Prayer," in *Works of Martin Luther*, volume 2 (Philadelphia: A.J. Holman Company, 1915).

"Lord's Prayer Explained," in *Luther's Catechetical Writings,* volume 1, translated by John Nicholas Lenker (Minneapolis: The Luther Press, 1907).

"Smalcald Articles," in *The Christian Book of Concord or Symbolical Works of the Evangelical Lutheran Church* (Newmarket: Solomon D. Henkel & Bros., 1854).

"Ninth Passion Sermon," in *Sermons on the Passion of Christ* (Rock Island, IL: Lutheran Augustana Book Concern, Schulze & Gassmann, 1871).

"Fourth Sunday After Trinity, Second Sermon, Romans 8:18–22, Redemption of Creatures," in *The Precious and*

Sacred Writings of Martin Luther, volume 8, translated by John Nicholas Lenker (Minneapolis: Lutherans in All Lands, 1908).

PHILIP MELANCHTHON (1497–1560)

Philip Melanchthon worked closely with Martin Luther as a professor, teacher, and theological thinker. He was one of the primary influences behind the landmark Augsburg Confession, and continued to help shape the Reformation's (and Luther's) doctrinal statements. He was by nature a moderator and a peacemaker—which proved to be an important, foundational role in the early years of the Reformation. Following a custom of the day, Melanchthon's great-uncle suggested he change his birth name, Philip Schwartzerdt ("black earth") to its Greek equivalent.

Sources Quoted

The Life of Philip Melanchthon, by Karl Friedrich Ledderhose and G. F. Krotel (Philadelphia: Lindsay & Blakiston, 1855).

Philip Melanchthon, the Protestant Preceptor of Germany, by James William Richard (New York; London: G.P. Putnam's Sons, 1902).

The Life of Philip Melanchthon, by Joseph Stump (Reading, PA; New York: Pilger Publishing House, 1897).

"To God Let All the Human Race" (Herr Gott dich loben alle wir), in *Psalmodia Germanica,* 2nd. ed. (The Liturgy and the Offices of Worship and Hymns of the American Province of the Unitas Fratrum, or the Moravian Church, 1908).

Marguerite de Navarre (1491–1549)

As a Renaissance woman, Marguerite de Navarre (Queen of Navarre, princess of France) was well educated in languages, philosophy, history, and theology—and eventually provided much the same education for her own daughter, Jeanne d'Albret (who would later became a Huguenot leader and mother of France's King Henry IV). She surrounded herself with many of the best thinkers and influencers of the day—including Protestants. As a writer, she produced volumes of verse and short stories, much of it with a spiritual theme. Her masterwork, called the *Heptameron,* remains popular even today. And as a Christian, she advocated for reform in the church, for a renewed focus on the Scriptures, and for Bible translation into French. Though not a Calvinist herself, she served as a mediator between Roman Catholics and Protestants (including John Calvin). It's thought she may have had a spiritual influence on the English Anne Boleyn, and she was certainly beloved in her own country.

Sources Quoted

Chansons Spirituelles, edited by Georges Dottin (Geneva: Droz, 1971).

The Primer of 1559

After the death of her half-sister Mary, Queen Elizabeth I came to the throne in the midst of a religious maelstrom. It seemed that Catholics, Anglicans, and independent Protestants had little upon which to agree. In response, the queen attempted in her own way to bring together the country's three major religious trends. Under the queen's authority, *The Primer of 1559* was assembled during those turbulent years, and included prayers dealing with a wide variety of topics, from peace to bedtime.

Sources Quoted

> *The Primer of 1559,* edited by John Wayland (London: 1559). Reprinted in *The Private Prayers of the Reign of Queen Elizabeth* (Cambridge: The Parker Society and University Press, 1851).

ROBERT ROLLOCK (1555–1599)

Robert Rollock is remembered primarily as a groundbreaking Reformation educator—the first regent and principal of the University of Edinburgh—but also as a theologian and a peacemaker within the young Scottish Reformed Church during the latter half of the sixteenth century. In the tumult of church and civic politics, he was especially known for gentleness and tact, and his teaching and writing (he wrote several well-received biblical commentaries) had a profound and lasting influence on Reformed covenant theology. He died at age forty-four.

Sources Quoted

> *Lectures, Upon the History of the Passion, Resurrection, and Ascension of Our Lord Jesus Christ* (Edinburgh: Andro Hart, 1616).

NICOLAUS SELNECKER (1532–1592)

Selnecker was born near Nürnberg and served as organist in Kaiserberg when he was only twelve years old. He attended the University of Wittenberg starting in 1550, where he became one of Philip Melanchthon's favorite students. He eventually graduated with a master's degree and went on to teach, even as a tutor to royalty. He was ordained in 1558, helped draft the Formula of Concord in 1577, and died in 1592. During his lifetime he produced a number of notable hymns, one of which is presented here as a prayer.

Sources Quoted

"Lord Jesu Christ, With Us Abide," 1587, translated by Catherine Winkworth, 1863. Published in 36 hymnals, including *Christian Worship Hymnal.*

Menno Simons (1496–1561)

Little is known about the early years of Menno Simons— except that he grew up in a poor peasant family in Friesland, Holland, during a bleak post-war period. Though he had originally never read the Bible, as a young man he trained for the priesthood, and was ordained in 1515 or 1516. After encountering the writings of Luther and Bullinger, however, and actually reading the Scriptures for himself, he began to question some of his traditionally held beliefs. Eventually he came to a crisis of faith when his brother Pieter was killed as an Anabaptist in 1535, and he left the priesthood the following year to join the same movement. Simons soon became its most influential leader and thinker, both in Holland and beyond, and many of the Anabaptists were even known by his name— Mennonites. He died twenty-five years after his break with the priesthood.

Sources Quoted

"On the Twenty-fifth Psalm," in *A Pleasing Meditation and Devout Contemplation* (Elkhart, Indiana: John F. Funk & Brother, 1871).

"A Brief and Clear Confession" and "The True Christian Faith," in *The Complete Works of Menno Simon* (Elkhart, Indiana: John F. Funk & Brother, 1871).

"Christian Baptism," in *A Plain Instruction from the Word of God, Concerning the Spiritual Resurrection and New or Heavenly Birth* (Elkhart, Indiana: John F. Funk and Brother, 1873).

HANS TAUSEN (1494–1561)

Hans Tausen is regarded as Denmark's leading Reformation-era theologian and change agent. After his studies he was ordained a Catholic priest, and was known early on for his skill as a linguist. He understood both Latin and Hebrew, and translated much of the Old Testament into Danish. His life dramatically changed, however, when he visited Wittenberg in 1523 to study and meet with Martin Luther. Returning to Denmark, he began preaching revolutionary Protestant doctrine— starting with his landmark sermon on Good Friday of 1525. Years of conflict followed between Catholic and Protestant factions, but he found favor among the people and protection from King Frederick I. Late in life, Tausen was appointed Bishop of Ribe.

Sources Quoted

> *Smaaskrifter af Hans Tausen*, portion translated by
> Robert Elmer (Copenhagen: Thieles Bogtrykkeri, 1870).

WILLIAM TYNDALE (1495–1536)

Tyndale was a biblical scholar and linguist who created
the first complete Bible translation into English from the
original Hebrew and Greek texts. His version was also the
first to use new printing press technology and the first to
use the word "Jehovah." Tyndale's work also had a lasting
impact on the English language; he introduced in his
translation a number of still-common phrases, including
"my brother's keeper," "salt of the earth," and "let there be
light." Later translators drew heavily on Tyndale's work
for the 1611 King James Version. But before that would
happen, Tyndale's opposition in 1530 to King Henry
VIII's divorce, on biblical grounds, prompted him to
flee England for Belgium. He was betrayed and captured
in 1535, convicted of heresy in 1536, and executed by
strangulation soon afterward. His dying prayer was "Lord!
Open the King of England's eyes." Tyndale has been
honored through the years for his influence on history,
and the Reformation, through films, documentaries, and
church commemorations.

Sources Quoted

> "Upon Matthew," in *The Works of the English Reformers:
> William Tyndale and John Frith*, volume 2, edited by
> Thomas Russell (London: Ebenezer Palmer, 1831).

Zacharias Ursinus (1534–1583)

Though he is seldom mentioned in lists of prominent reformers, Zacharias Ursinus should be remembered as one of the primary authors of the Heidelberg Catechism— still used and appreciated in many congregations today. His prayer here is from the commentary he wrote on the catechism. He was born in Breslau (now Poland), studied in Wittenberg, and taught for a time in Breslau before moving to Heidelberg to lead the theological academy there. He often worked closely with his friend and mentor, Peter Martyr Vermigli, and promoted Vermigli's *Loci*. Ursinus's behind-the-scenes work as a theologian and writer did much to define the Reformed movement for centuries to come.

Sources Quoted

> *The Commentary of Dr. Zacharias Ursinus on the Heidelberg Catechism,* translated by G.W. Williard (Cincinnati: Elm Street Printing Co., 1888).

Peter Martyr Vermigli (1499–1562)

Peter Martyr Vermigli occupies a unique position as one of the most overlooked but influential figures of the Reformation. He's sometimes called "The Italian Calvin," but, as one biographer noted, it might be more accurate to call Calvin "The French Vermigli." He entered the Augustinian order at age fifteen, and quickly rose to become a traveling lecturer, priest, and abbot. He excelled at the deepest levels of scholarship, learning Latin, Greek, and Hebrew. But while serving as abbot in Naples, he became convinced of the scriptural principle of justification by faith alone—a principle which would guide the remainder of his life. Eventually he would have no choice but to renounce his vows and flee Catholic Italy. From there he taught Old Testament in Strasbourg and married a former nun before receiving an invitation in 1547 to help Thomas Cranmer build the fledgling Church of England by teaching at Oxford. While there he helped to revise the Book of Common Prayer, as well as create the authoritative Forty-Two Articles, and helped with the reformation of ecclesiastical laws. Vermigli continued as a leading voice of the Reformation through his writing, teaching, and debates until his death in Zürich at age sixty-three.

Sources Quoted

Common Places, translated by Anthonie Marten (Greenwich: 1583).

John Wycliffe (1331–1384)

No account of the Reformation is complete without mention of the "Morningstar of the Reformation," John Wycliffe (or Wyclif, or Wickliffe). As a theologian, Oxford professor, reformer, priest, and Bible translator, few had more influence on the church of his day—and beyond. His views on predestination, veneration of the saints, the mass and the papacy, the priesthood, the presence of Christ in communion, and much more would influence the philosophy and teachings of reformers who would follow his lead in centuries to come. And like the later reformers, he regarded the Bible as the only authoritative guide in faith. He is perhaps best known today for his advocacy for and work in translating the Bible into common vernacular (in his case, English). The Council of Constance declared him a heretic in 1415, some thirty years after his death.

Sources Quoted

Writings of the Reverend and Learned John Wickliff, first American edition (Philadelphia: Presbyterian Board of Publication, 1842).

Tracts and Treatises of John de Wycliffe, with Selections and Translations from His Manuscripts and Latin Works (London: Wycliffe Society, 1845).

Huldrych Zwingli (1484–1531)

As one of the most prominent Swiss Reformation leaders of his time, Zwingli startled his Zürich congregation by preaching through the entire book of Matthew (and eventually the entire New Testament) in 1519. It was a radical departure; up to that time, expository preaching of that kind was unheard of. His ideas for church reform eventually came to the attention of Martin Luther, since both men held similar positions regarding clerical marriage, customs like fasting, images in the church, and corruption. Unfortunately, the two men could never agree on the meaning of communion. Zwingli also fiercely opposed the Anabaptist reformers, and his opposition to holdout Swiss Catholic cantons led to his eventual death on the battlefield in 1531.

Sources Quoted

"Archeteles: Reply to Bishop's Admonition" in *The Latin Works and The Correspondence of Huldreich Zwingli*, volume 1, edited by Samuel Macauley Jackson

(New York: G. P. Putnam's Sons; London: The Knickerbocker Press, 1912).

"A Christian Song Written by Huldreich Zwingli When He Was Attacked by the Pestilence (end of 1519)," in *The Latin Works and The Correspondence of Huldreich Zwingli*, volume 1, edited by Samuel Macauley Jackson (New York: G. P. Putnam's Sons; London: The Knickerbocker Press, 1912).

"Exposition of the Christian Faith," in *The Latin Works of Huldreich Zwingli*, volume 2, edited by Samuel Macauley Jackson (Philadelphia: The Heidelberg Press, 1922).

Index of Authors and Sources

Henry Airay   53, 63, 119, 134–35, 142, 197, 321

Lancelot Andrewes   14, 17, 29, 32, 37, 65, 67, 101, 107, 109, 117, 163, 219, 221, 261, 273, 291, 293, 297, 301, 311, 313, 321–22

Thomas Becon   89, 131, 135, 160, 163, 172, 185, 189–90, 211, 294, 306, 322–23

Theodore Beza   27, 323

Georg Blaurock   91, 323–24

A Book of Christian Prayers   24, 59, 155, 171, 214–15, 261–62, 276, 295, 324–25

John Bradford   17, 21, 25–26, 29, 31, 54–55, 57, 69, 103, 107, 133, 165, 185, 191, 209, 217, 225, 229, 263, 268, 275, 277, 279, 295, 300, 305, 307, 314–15, 325–26

Martin Bucer   167, 289, 326

Heinrich Bullinger   61, 139, 171, 205, 283, 319, 326–27

John Calvin	12–13, 46, 50, 52–53, 57, 60–61, 75, 77, 81, 83, 87–89, 91, 95, 105, 115, 125, 136, 139, 149, 155, 164–65, 167, 193–95, 201, 215, 269, 277, 319, 327–28
Myles Coverdale	51, 59, 63, 97, 121, 127, 132–33, 145, 157–58, 162, 186, 211, 233, 237, 241, 281, 285, 319, 329
Thomas Cranmer	112, 141, 177, 181, 187, 266, 288, 290, 330
Elisabeth Cruciger	20, 331
John Downame	42, 179, 331–32
Guillaume (William) Farel	205, 253, 319, 332
Anna of Freiberg	75, 332–33
Johann Gerhard	19, 93, 111, 113, 115, 118, 129, 136, 143, 145, 147, 283, 333
Lady Jane Grey	151, 334
Niels Hemmingsen	31, 86, 126, 153, 169, 177, 207, 217, 281, 334–35

Balthasar Hubmaier

21, 37, 39–41, 43, 45, 47,
48, 119, 203, 335–36

John Knox

27, 140, 173, 176, 222,
239, 255, 257, 270, 300,
304, 336–37

Martin Luther

58, 72–73, 83–84, 85, 95,
117, 202, 227, 229, 231,
233, 235, 237–38, 243,
253, 265, 271, 284, 289,
304–5, 311, 319, 337–39

Philip Melanchthon

105, 201, 203, 252,
339–40

Marguerite de Navarre

269, 340

The Primer of 1559

77, 94, 97, 137–38, 170,
180, 189, 259, 263, 265,
273, 293, 307, 315–17,
340–41

Robert Rollock

137, 143, 191, 197, 341

Nicholaus Selnecker

313, 341–42

Menno Simons

38, 44, 85, 93, 108, 125,
149, 161, 166, 168, 173,
175, 207, 248, 249, 251,
274, 342–43

Hans Tausen

33, 258, 343–44

William Tyndale   87, 101, 146, 235, 344

Zacharius Ursinus   245, 345

Peter Martyr Vermigli   175, 178–79, 257, 345–46

John Wycliffe   12, 62, 73, 156, 196,
                               346–47

Huldrych Zwingli   15, 80–81, 193, 208,
                               347–48